GREECE

A Biblical Tour of Greek Historical Sites

77 Insights into Ancient Greek Culture
that Make the New Testament Come Alive

COSTAS TSEVAS

WITH ERIC LARSON

ILLUSTRATED BY MARGIE ANDERSON

GREECE
A Biblical Tour of Greek Historical Sites

Printed in the United States

ISBN 978-1-61715-582-6

First printing, 2022

A Note to Readers

There are two trips included on every serious Bible reader's bucket list.

One is to Israel, to visit the land of the Old Testament and tour the country where Jesus lived, worked and died. The other is to Greece—to walk in Paul's footsteps, town after town, through the book of Acts—where, thanks to all those hard-digging archaeological folks, you can actually stand on the very ground where Paul once stood (wow).

This book is a guide for your Greece trip.

Our purpose is simple. Through a series of short stories, verses, images and maps, we'll introduce you to things you might learn on a guided tour of biblical sites in Greece—that is, if your renowned tour guide is Costas Tsevas. The 77 neatly-packaged teachings in this book are *his* commentaries—*his* mini-lectures, so to speak.

Thus, the tour language you're about to encounter ("From Delphi, we head to Athens...") are words you might hear Costas speak as you board the bus, pen in hand, eager to reach your next destination.

And whether you take this book along on an actual tour of Greece or choose to travel there vicariously from the comfort of your favorite couch, this guide *will* help you understand your Bible better.

So, sit back, relax and enjoy your journey!

Kaló taxídi!

Eric Larson
Salinas
2022

Table of Contents

Plato and Aristotle have had a great work appointed to them, not only as the heathen pioneers of the Truth before it was revealed, but as educators of Christian minds in every age.

The former enriched human thought with appropriate ideas for the reception of the highest truth in its highest form; the latter mapped out all the provinces of human knowledge, that Christianity might visit them and bless them.

Conybeare and Howson

The divine light, we are told, "lighteneth every man." We should, therefore, expect to find in the imagination of the great Pagan teachers and myth makers some glimpse of that theme which we believe to be the very plot of the whole cosmic story—the theme of incarnation, death, and rebirth.

C.S. Lewis

Turn away from these vain things to the living God, who made the heaven and the earth and the sea and everything in them, who in past generations allowed all the nations to walk in their own ways; yet he did not leave himself without witness, for he did good, giving you rains from heaven and fruitful seasons, filling your hearts with food and gladness.

Acts 14:15-17

The Ancient World

He has made everything beautiful in its time. Also, he has put eternity in their hearts... **Ecclesiastes 3:11** (NKJV)

Before we begin our biblical tour of Greece, it will be helpful to set the stage for our journey by talking about how God worked in the ancient world to prepare the way for the coming of Christ. In this chapter, after introducing God's work with Israel and the nations, we'll meet special king-priests and explore two major Greek miracles that radically changed the world.

Italy
Greece
Mediterranean Sea

The Mediterranean World

The Nations

Who in past generations allowed all the **nations** to walk in their own ways; yet he did not leave himself without witness, for he did good, giving you rains from heaven and fruitful seasons, filling your hearts with food and gladness.

Acts 14:16–17

❧❧❧

Nations: (ETH'NOS 'έθνος) *n.*
Gentiles, peoples, ethnic groups

God Loved These People, Too

Let's start this story from the beginning.

The most important event that ever took place on this Earth was the coming of Jesus Christ, the Son of God. For this reason, God prepared the world to receive him.

He accomplished this by working in two directions at the same time. While he prepared Israel for the *coming* of the Messiah, he also made the nations ready to receive the *message* of the Messiah.

Said another way, while God's purpose with Israel was to create the *content* of the gospel, his purpose among the nations was to build the *container* for the gospel. And as we'll soon discover, God began his work among the nations centuries before he called Abraham.

In Acts 14, the Apostle Paul says that though God permitted the nations go their own ways, he never stopped loving them and witnessing himself to them by doing good things for them, like sending them rain from above. This means that in antiquity, in the fallen world into which the nations came, the Creator declared himself to people through the beauty, order and power of nature (Psalm 19:1).

The purpose of this witness was to awaken the nations and testify to them that all human beings, regardless of their origins, can find God and be reconciled to him if they earnestly seek after him (Acts 10:35).

Israel could neither understand nor accept the fact that God could love the nations too (Acts 11:1-9). To strict Jews, the Gentiles were like chaff to be burned. Yet, remarkably, God would use the Jews to carry his message of salvation to the non-Jewish world.

At the same time, God also used the other Mediterranean peoples, especially the Greeks. They became the agents through which he would create the principles, ideas, language and culture that were needed to effectively communicate his message.

As a result, in the fullness of the times, when the first Hebrew disciples of Christ took the good news of the gospel to the world, their mission field was already cultivated and waiting to be sown.

Two Relationships

Ask and it will be given to you, **seek** and you will find, knock and it will be opened for you. For everyone who asks receives, and everyone who **seeks** finds... **Matthew** 7:7–8

❧❧❧

Seek: (ZETE'O ζητέω) *v.*
to search intensely for something

Ask and Receive, Seek and Find

In the generations before the coming of Christ, since the nations and Israel played unique roles in God's unfolding drama of redemption, the nature of their relationships with God differed. While Israel knew God's presence *directly* through his words and deeds (Heb 3:7-9), God revealed himself to the nations *indirectly* through nature (Rom 1:20).

These different roles required in two different ways by which these peoples approached God. For the children of Israel—those under his divine direction—theirs was to *ask* of God in order to *receive* from him. But the nations' mandate was to *seek* God in order to *find* him.

We find examples of both *asking* and *seeking* in the Bible. As Moses prepared the Israelites to enter the Good Land, he warned them not to leave God's presence to worship idols. If this occurs, said Moses, God will remove you from the land and scatter you among the nations. But if "from there" you *seek* the Lord, you will *find* him—just as the nations do—if you *search* for him with all of your heart (Deut 4:25-29).

In the New Testament, Matthew opens his gospel with just such a *search*. There we find Magi coming from the East, following a star, *seeking* the one who was born King of the Jews. And when they *find* the young child, they fall down and worship him (Matt 2:1-12).

And 30 years later, when Jesus began his ministry by turning over tables, the Jews *asked* him, "What sign can you *show us* to prove your authority to do this?" (John 2:18). They wanted to *receive* an answer.

Paul speaks to both of these approaches when he explains to the Corinthian believers that while the Jews *ask* for a sign, the Greeks *seek* wisdom. For Jews, miracles come from God and are to be *received*. For Greeks, labor and discovery are required (1 Cor 1:22-23).

As we'll soon see, during the 6th century BC, there were people in the Mediterranean world who laid aside the myths and vain religions of their times and *sought* to discover the origin of nature. Over the decades, their diligent *search* for truth led first to the development of thought and eventually led them to *find* the one true God.

The King-Priests

Then Melchizedek **king** of Salem brought out bread and wine; he was the **priest** of God Most High. And he blessed him and said: "Blessed be Abram of God Most High, Possessor of heaven and earth."... and (Abram) gave him a tithe of all.

Genesis 14:18–20 (NKJV)

❧❧❧

King: (BASIL'EUS βασιλεύς) *n.*
a monarch, decision maker

Priest: (HIEREUS' 'ιερεύς) *n.*
an intermediary who offers sacrifices

A Gentile King–Priest Blesses Abram

One way that God worked among the nations was to establish the institution of the king-priest. The history of European civilization dates back to the Minoan culture late in the 3rd millennium before Christ. At that time, the Minoans had created a vast peaceful empire across the Aegean region centered on the island of Crete. They were the first culture we know of that was ruled by king-priests.

King-priests (*wanax* in Greek) were both rulers of their societies and high priests of their religions. And unlike the Pharaohs in Egypt or kings of Babylon, these ancient rulers never considered themselves as gods to be worshipped.

The king-priests ruled the Minoans and the Myceneans that came after them for 1,000 years before Israel's first king and for 500 years before its first priest. And while Israel's priests came from one tribe and its kings from another, the ancient king-priesthood combined both of these offices in one person. This never happened in the history of Israel.

Melchizedek, a Gentile king-priest, is mentioned in the Bible in Genesis and in Hebrews. This unique person, who was both the King of Salem and Priest of God Most High (Heb 7:1) was already ruling in Canaan when Abram arrived. And as a Gentile who believed in God as the Creator of the natural world, Melchizedek blessed Abram in the name of the "Possessor of heaven and earth" (Gen 14:18-20).

In Hebrews, Melchizedek pre-figures Jesus Christ, since, like the ancient king-priests, Christ is *both* our King and our High Priest (Heb 7:3). And according to 1 Peter 2:9, because of our union with Christ, we believers are called a "royal priesthood"—king-priests.

Here in Greece, king-priests ruled continuously from these early days until the time of Alexander the Great. Athens was governed by such persons. The Acropolis was their palace sanctuary.

Against this backdrop, to accomplish his purposes, God performed two major miracles. The first miracle was Athenian democracy. The second was a person—Alexander the Great.

The First Greek Miracle

What is **man** that you take thought for him, or the son of man, that you care for him? You made him for a little while lower than the angels. **Hebrews 2:6–7**

ॐ ॐ ॐ

Man: (ANTH'ROPOS 'άνθρωπος) *n.*
a human being

Every Human Life Matters

During the 7th century BC, after the reign of Codros, the king-priest of Athens, the role of the monarchy began to change when the office of the king-priest became an elected position.

When that happened, groups of nobles, called "royal committees," gradually took over the administration of the city. And for the first time in human history, ruling power passed from one person to a group of people (the *oligarchia* in Greek).

This new political system, called oligarchy, governed Athens for a time until tyrants took control of the city and a period of severe social disruption ensued. Over time, powerful Athenian families rose up and began to promote their own rulers, and a civil war nearly broke out.

In the midst of this chaotic situation, a man named Cleisthenes stepped forward. He gathered all of the men of Athens over 20 years old into the town square and said to them, "Look, it's a pity for us to kill each other when we could sit down, discuss our common problems and find solutions together." Everyone agreed.

So, from this group of common, ordinary citizens, "the assembly of Athens" was formed and became the highest governing authority of the city. When this body (*demas* in Greek) began to execute its new-found power (*kratos* in Greek), the world's first *demo-cracy* was born.

This novel political/social system with its new principles brought an explosion of science, arts and humanities to Athens and launched a new era, known as "classical culture." In this culture, the citizen, the simple human being, became the most valuable element of society and "the measure of all things." As part of the collective body, every human life mattered.

Through this miracle of Athenian democracy, God succeeded in laying the groundwork for his message of the gospel. Christ would soon come to give meaning to every person's life. He himself would be the prize, the treasure for each earthen vessel (2 Cor 4:7).

The Second Greek Miracle

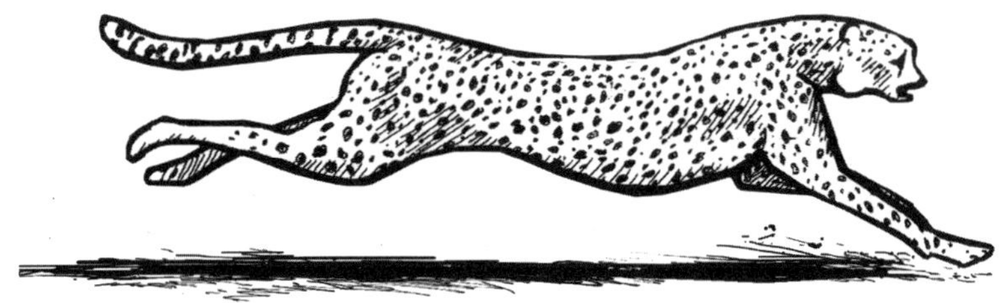

And four great beasts came up from the sea... (one was) like
a **leopard**. **Daniel** 7:**3,6** (NKJV)

❧❧❧

Leopard: (PAR'DALIS παρδάλις) *n.* a leopard

Alexander Spread Greek Culture Everywhere

Athenian democracy and the classical culture that was born in Athens was a miracle. But this unique democratic system lasted only 50 years and was never repeated again. Yet through its principles, God had transformed the Mediterranean world and had prepared its people to receive the message of the gospel.

Then, almost a century and a half later, we have a second miracle, and this miracle is a person, Alexander the Great. Alexander became king in 336 BC following the assassination of his father. He was only 20 years old when this crazy young boy, with a group of about 40,000 men, attacked and defeated the Persian empire, the superpower of that time, with its army of 1.7 million trained soldiers. That was a miracle.

But the details of this second miracle didn't stop there. Alexander didn't have a professional army. His volunteers were common Greeks—teachers, artisans, historians—who had left their jobs to join in his campaign. Yet, over the next 13 years, with the speed of a leopard (as prophesied by Daniel), this ragtag military force conquered the world and spread Greek culture all the way to India. That was a miracle too.

Everywhere they went, the Greeks built new cities—hundreds of them. Seventy were named Alexandria in honor of Alexander. Many were built in Palestine. In the New Testament, a cluster of ten Greek cities became known as "the Decapolis" (*deca* ten, *polis* city).

At Jesus' time, one of these ten, Scythopolis, was located only 13 miles southeast of Nazareth, his hometown. Sepphoris, the capital of Galilee, was also built by the Greeks and was in walking distance of Jesus' home.

Alexander died in 323 BC when he was only 33 years old. But he left behind a completely new world, called "the Hellenistic world." For the first time in history, the entire Mediterranean region spoke one common language (Greek), shared a common culture and used a common monetary system.

The stage was set for the coming of Christ.

The Greek Language

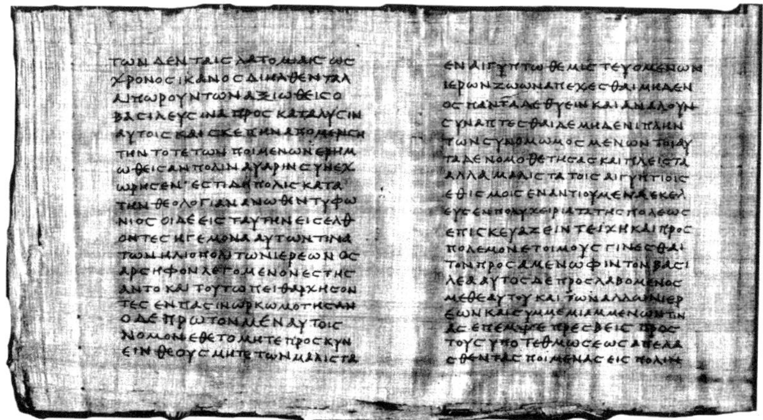

And Pilate wrote an inscription and fastened it to the cross... and it was written in Hebrew, in Latin, and in **Greek**.

John 19:19-20

❧❧❧

in Greek: (HELLENISTI' Ἑλληνιστί) *adv.*
in the Hellenistic language

The Language of the New Testament

Before Jesus was born, Alexander and the Greek rulers who succeeded him made a deliberate effort to "Hellenize" the entire Mediterranean world, including Israel, with their principles, language and culture.

When the Romans came to power, they were fascinated by this culture—so much so that they adopted much of it as their own. Greek gods became Roman gods with new names; Greek city centers (*agoras*) became Roman forums; and Greek became the language of the Empire.

Greek also became the language of the New Testament. At Jesus' time, the Jews living in Israel were bilingual. Though their mother tongue was Aramaic, a dialect related to Hebrew, the Jews also knew Greek, the language of the Gentiles, the vernacular of business.

Jesus, his disciples and the Apostle Paul would all have been fluent in Greek and would have used the Septuagint, the Greek version of the Old Testament, translated from Hebrew hundreds of years earlier. All of the books of the New Testament were written in Greek and their quotes from the Old Testament came primarily from the Septuagint.

Three elements—Jewish religion, Roman rule and Greek culture—converged to form the context of the New Testament world. All three played important roles in informing the New Testament text.

Greek culture showed up in the New Testament in three ways. First, the legends of Greek *mythology* created powerful illustrations of divine realities and a number of mythological characters, like Asclepius or Apollo, prefigured Jesus Christ himself.

Second, Greek *political institutions*, like Athenian democracy or king-priests, modeled characteristics for both the believers and the church and introduced unique terminology—*logos, ekklesia*—into the biblical text.

And third, Greek *philosophy*, from the ancient observers of nature up to Socrates and his disciples, contributed the thoughts and ideas that created the conceptual frameworks that help us understand New Testament truth.

The Gospel Comes West

In the fullness of time, God sent his Son into this world to redeem mankind from our sins through Jesus' death and resurrection. Then, on the day of Pentecost, shortly after Christ ascended back to heaven, the church was born, and the church age began.

In his New Testament book of Acts, Luke chronicles the history of the early church, telling the story of how the gospel spread throughout the Mediterranean world. He begins his account by describing how the good news first came to the Jews, primarily through Peter's ministry, starting in Jerusalem before fanning out across Israel's provinces of Judea, Samaria and Galilee.

Then, beginning in chapter 13, the focus shifts to the nations, as Paul and his co-workers take the message of Christ to the peoples living outside of Israel through a series of missionary journeys.

Our interest in this unfolding story centers on Paul's second trip through the Gentile world as he, Silas and Timothy bring the gospel west through Asia Minor (today's Turkey). across the Aegean Sea to the port of Neapolis in Greece.

This is where our biblical tour begins.

In the rest of this book, we will follow Paul and his team through Acts chapters 16-18 as they bring God's message of salvation to the Greek cities of Philippi, Thessalonica, Berea, Athens and Corinth before they depart for home from the Corinthian port of Cenchrea.

Along the way, we will also visit four places that are not found in Acts—Vergina, Meteora, Delphi and Eleusis—where we will discover important historical, cultural things that have informed and enriched the writing of the New Testament.

Paul's Journey and Our Tour

Following Paul's Footsteps

The map on the opposite page shows the path that Paul and his party followed through today's Greece during his second missionary journey. For the purpose of creating context, we have superimposed his route onto a recent political map of countries in this region.

Tours of Greece that "follow in Paul's Footsteps" often trace his movements chronologically as presented in the book of Acts. Here is a summary of the places Paul visited during this mission to Europe.

1. Paul and his party sail from Troas in Asia Minor	Acts 16:11
2. They overnight on the island of Samothrace	Acts 16:11
3. They set foot in Greece at the port of Neapolis	Acts 16:11
4. They go inland to the village of Philippi	Acts 16:12
5. After staying a while, they walk to Thessalonica	Acts 17:1
6. From Thessalonica, they journey on to Berea	Acts 17:10
7. Paul's life is threatened. He escapes to Athens	Acts 17:14
8. After his stay in Athens, he goes to Corinth	Acts 18:1
9. He remains in Corinth for a year and a half	Acts 18:11
10. Then, he heads home from the port of Cenchrea	Acts 18:18

Philippi

From Paul and Timothy, servants of Christ Jesus, to all the saints in Christ Jesus who are in **Philippi**... Grace to you and peace from God our Father and the Lord Jesus Christ.

Philippians 1:1

Our tour following Paul's footsteps through Greece begins in Philippi. In this chapter, after setting the stage for Paul's arrival in Europe, we will visit "Lydia's River," outside of town, before exploring one of the most important archaeological sites for Christians to visit in the world.

The Four Districts of Macedonia

Archaeological Site at Philippi

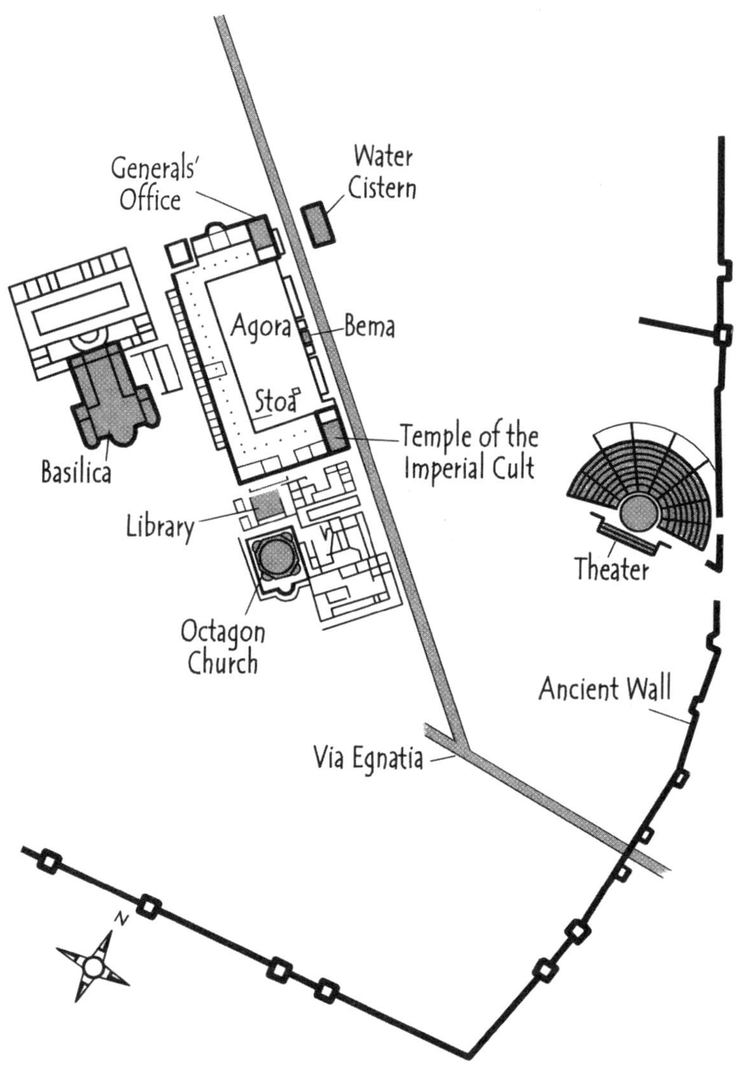

Macedonia

And a vision in the night appeared to Paul; a man of **Macedonia** was standing there, urging him and saying, "Come over to **Macedonia** and help us!" **Acts 16:9**

~ ~ ~

Macedonia: (MAKEDONI'A Μακεδονία) *n.*
a province of the Roman Empire

Paul Visits the Place of the Tall People

In the years following the death of Alexander, his four leading generals fought among themselves as they divided up his empire. And while their struggles dragged on for generations, Greek culture and language spread rapidly across the region.

Two centuries later, when the Romans conquered the world, they created provinces, sub-provinces and districts in the occupied countries as governmental administrative units.

At Paul's time, Macedonia, located in the northern half of today's Greece, was one of these provinces. The smaller province of Achaia occupied much of the southern part of the country (see the map on page 34).

Centuries earlier, the original kingdom of Macedonia had been established in this region by Perdiccas of Macedon. The kingdom grew rapidly in power and influence under Alexander's father, King Philip. Then, when Philip died, Alexander expanded Macedonia's influence across the eastern Mediterranean world.

Almost every Greek name has a meaning, and Macedonia is no exception. The word literally means, "the place of the tall people." It's possible that in ancient times the southern Greeks were shorter than the northern Greeks. This is because the northern Greeks were called, *makedhos*, "the tall ones." It was in this "place of the tall people" that the Apostle Paul would begin to preach the gospel of Christ in Europe.

Luke's record of Paul's first visit to Macedonia and Achaia begins at Acts 16:8, where we learn that, after being directed by the Holy Spirit to pass through Asia Minor (today's Turkey), Paul and his co-workers arrived at the city of Troas on the coast of the Aegean Sea.

There, Paul saw a vision during the night of a "man of Macedonia" crying out for help. After concluding that God was sending him to Macedonia to preach the gospel, Paul and his party, which now included Luke himself, answered God's call and set sail across the Aegean bound for another continent.

Neapolis

And when Paul had seen the vision, immediately **we** tried to go into Macedonia, concluding that God had called us to **preach the gospel** to them. So, setting sail from Troas, **we** sailed on a direct course to Samothrace, and on the following day to Neapolis. **Acts 16:10-11**

❧❧❧

Preach the gospel: (EUANGELI'ZŌ ε'υαγγελείζω) *v.* evangelize, announce the good news

Paul's Party Sets Foot on European Soil

After stopping overnight on the island of Samothrace, Paul stepped on continental European soil for the first time when his ship reached the port of Neapolis on the following day. That's when this "new city" (*neos* new *polis* city) became the gospel's gateway to the Western world.

Neapolis was founded in the 7th century BC by the Thasians, people who lived on the nearby island of Thasos, two miles off the coast of Greece. These people were famous ship builders and built this little seaport as a place to transfer the pine wood they gathered from the mainland to their island for their ships.

Some years later, while the Thasians were searching the hills near Neapolis for high quality wood, they discovered gold deposits. They decided to build a second town closer to the gold and negotiated with the local people to do so. Because this town was near an underground water supply, they called it "Springs."

In 356 BC, a dispute arose between the Thasians in Springs and the locals over nearby cultivated lands. King Philip II was asked to resolve the dispute. When he found the gold, he kicked the Thasians out, remodeled the town and renamed it Philippi after himself.

In the 8th century AD, when Philippi was destroyed, many of its inhabitants moved to Neapolis. As the city grew, it became a Christian center, as Philippi had been years before. For this reason, the residents changed its name to Christopolis, "the City of Christ."

Neapolis bore this name until the 15th century when the Ottoman army came and settled their cavalry there. Appropriately, they renamed the city Kavala, its modern name.

The Roman road, Via Egnatia, connected Neapolis with Philippi and would have been the road Paul walked on when he traveled inland from the seaport. Visitors to Kavala can still walk on this road today.

The Village of Philippi

And from thence to Philippi, which is **the chief city** of that part of Macedonia, and a **colony.** **Acts 16:11–12** KJV

And from there we went to Philippi, which is **a city colony of the first district** of Macedonia. **Acts 16:11–12** Greek

❧❧❧

Colony: (KOLONI'A κολωνία) *n.*
a Roman town, a miniature Rome

A Small Colony—Not "The Chief City"

The years that followed the Roman invasion of Macedonia were troubled times. Quite often, the Macedonians organized rebellions against their unwanted visitors. For this reason, the Romans divided Macedonia into four smaller districts (page 34) and placed restrictions on the people. For a time, residents of one district were not allowed to communicate with, marry or do business with those of other districts.

The Romans gave each district its own name, number and capital. District number one was *Eastern Macedonia*. Its capital was the city of Amphipolis. District number two, *Central Macedonia*, had as its capital Thessalonica, which was also the capital of the entire province.

Western Macedonia, the third district, was home to Mount Olympus and had the city of Pella as its capital. Pella was also the capital of the ancient kingdom of Macedonia and the birthplace of Alexander. District number four was *Northern Macedonia* with the city of Heraclea as its capital.

Philippi was a small farming village located in Macedonia's first district. In 42 BC, a famous Roman battle took place nearby as Mark Antony and Octavian's armies fought against the armies of Brutus and Cassius in the plains south of town.

When the war ended, as a reward for their faithful service, the Roman commanders gave their retired veterans plots of farmland near Philippi, and the town became a Roman colony. At Paul's time, a colony was like a miniature Rome. The city was governed by Roman law, used Latin as its primary language and held Roman currency.

In Acts 16:11-12, the unfortunate wording of the King James Version makes Philippi seem much more important than it really was. First, Philippi was not "the chief city" of that part of Macedonia – that was Amphipolis, the capital of the province. Also, according to history and to the literal Greek text of the New Testament, Philippi was a very small town, "a city colony of the first district of Macedonia."

Lydia's River

And on the Sabbath day we went outside the gate to the riverside, where we thought there would be a place of prayer, and we sat down and spoke to the women who had gathered there. And a certain woman named Lydia, a **seller of purple cloths** from the city of Thyatira, a worshipper of God, listened. **Acts 16:13–14**

Seller of purple: (PORPHUROP'OLIS πορφυρόπωλις) *n.*
female trader of purple goods

The Macedonian Man Was an Asian Woman!

Wherever Paul traveled, he seemed to be well informed about the location of scattered Jewish populations.

When Paul came to Philippi, since there was no synagogue in town, he knew that there must be a very small Jewish community. According to Jewish law, a place had to have a minimum of ten Jewish men in order to have a synagogue. Because of this requirement, the few faithful Jews in town met outside the city walls by the river for prayers.

This is where Paul and his party went on the Sabbath, and this is where our tour of Philippi begins, on the banks of the Zygakti River, a place commonly known as "Lydia's River".

When Paul reached the river, he found a group of women gathered there. So, he and his co-workers sat down and began to speak with them. One of these women was Lydia, a businesswoman from the city of Thyatira in Asia Minor, a seller of purple goods. When the Lord opened her heart to hear Paul's speaking, Lydia became the first Christian convert in Europe. In a word, the Macedonian man Paul had seen in his vision turned out to be an Asian woman!

Do you know how cloth merchants made purple dye in those days? The purple color came from a few drops of a liquid produced by the snails who lived in sea shells found in the Eastern Mediterranean. Hundreds of snails were required to make the dye for one garment. And while this liquid dye worked well on animal fabrics like wool or silk, it did not work on plant-based fabrics like linen or cotton.

Because the dyeing process was complicated, purple garments were very expensive. For this reason, over time, purple became the color of royal families and rulers. In the Bible, the rich man in Luke 16:19 was clothed in "purple and fine linen." And Roman soldiers put a purple robe on Jesus, mocking him as "King of the Jews" (John 19:2).

Purple also became the official imperial color of the Romans, which is probably the main reason why Lydia came to Philippi, a Roman colony, to sell her purple goods.

The Theater

So the city was filled with the confusion, and they rushed with a single purpose into the **theater**, dragging with them Gaius and Aristarchus, Macedonians, traveling-companions of Paul.

Acts 19:29

ᘐᘐᘐ

Theater: (THE'ATRON θέατρον) *n.*
a place for viewing a show from a distance

Theos, Tragedy and Comedy

The archaeological site in Philippi is located a short distance from "Lydia's River." Our tour of this site begins at the theater, one of the oldest monuments of the site, built on a hillside overlooking the town.

In Greek, the word for theater (*theatron*) has the same root as *theos*, the Greek word for God. Both come from *thea*, a term which means to view something in a panoramic, widescreen way—to see the big picture clearly without being distracted by the details. To the ancient Greeks, this big picture perspective was how the gods viewed them, and to Greek theatergoers, this is how they watched their plays.

The theater, a half-circle structure with a stage, first appeared in Athens during the time of the Athenian democracy. But it was not an institution created solely for amusement. Instead, it was more like a school for adults that taught ethics and morals, twin foundations of democracy. People attended theaters to learn morality through drama.

Greek dramas evolved in two directions into what we call *tragedy* and *comedy*. *Tragedies* were plays that demonstrated how piety is the way to develop ethics and morals in society. Playwrights told the stories of famous Greek "hubrists"—arrogant, overconfident people, who did things that challenged the gods. These plays portrayed acts of hubris on stage and demonstrated the divine dislike for such attitudes through the curses which soon fell upon the offenders.

The other type of drama was *comedy*, a type of play that showed spectators who they really were—not who they thought they were – by holding a mirror up in front of them through the use of sarcasm and satire. The *comedies* fulfilled the Greek saying, "Know thyself."

When the Romans invaded Greece, they brought with them their gladiators, beasts and bloody shows. Theaters soon became convenient venues for these events. Since the Romans had no use for the stages, they removed them and closed the circle of the building, thereby doubling the seating capacity. This was the origin of the *amphitheater*, a word which literally means, "double theater."

The Agora

When her owners saw that their hope of profit was gone, they seized Paul and Silas and dragged them into the **marketplace** before the rulers. **Acts 16:19**

❧❧❧

Marketplace: (AGORA' 'αγορά) *n.*
the town square, city center, social hub

So Much More Than a Marketplace

Down below the theater, in the excavated area of the archaeological site, there is a very special place. This wide-open space is the *agora*, the rectangular city center of Philippi.

When Paul visited this town, the *agora* was a cleared, level but unpaved area surrounded by buildings on three sides. Standing above the *agora* and looking down on it, the administrative section of the city occupied the end on the right, while the cultural and the religious sections were located on the opposite end on the left (see page 35).

Since the *agora* was the place where the townspeople gathered for social and public events, a covered porch (*stoa*) was built along the entire length of the longer side across the square to provide shade from the sun and protection from the rain.

The commercial shops that filled the spaces behind the *stoa* were places where people could buy food, clothing and other things. This might be why *agora* is translated, "marketplace" in many English Bibles. But this town square was so much more than a marketplace.

In the story told by Luke in Acts 16:16-24, Paul caused an uproar in Philippi when he cast a demon out of a slave girl. Most Bible versions suggest that the slave girl's owners seized Paul and dragged him into "the marketplace" to face the authorities of the city. Yet, wouldn't it be strange to imagine that they dragged Paul into a shopping center?

The English term, *agoraphobia*, is not the fear of buying and selling things. No. *Agoraphobia* is the fear of meeting other people in public, open spaces—a phobia of going to the *agora*.

This broader understanding of the *agora* brings new meaning to this word's usage in the New Testament. Jesus would have been very familiar with *agoras*. He spoke of them frequently in the Gospels.

They were the places where day laborers could be hired (Matt 20:3), where proud Pharisees could be seen and receive greetings (Luke 11:43), where folks could bring their sick for healing (Mark 6:56) and where children could play and call to their friends (Luke 7:32).

The Bema

For we must all appear before the **judgment seat** of Christ, so that each one may be repaid according to what he has done while in the body, whether good or bad. **2 Corinthians 5:10**

❧❧❧

Judgment seat: (BE′MA βήμα) *n.*
a raised platform, a grandstand

The Public Place for Reward or Shame

At the center of the open side of the *agora* stand the remains of a very important part of this town square. The raised, rectangular platform that was built here is what most English Bibles call the "judgment seat" or "tribunal." The word in Greek is *bema*. This was the podium from which, during Roman times, the local Roman authorities would participate in public events held in the *agora*.

Much like U.S. Presidents sit in grandstands to watch parades on the 4th of July, the Romans would watch ceremonies, announce new laws or publicly reward local Greek benefactors from the *bema*.

Incidentally, most Greeks considered these benefactors traitors.

But the *bema* was more widely known for something else. It was the place where accused revolutionaries or those who had insulted Rome were brought to be judged. In this most public part of the *agora*, those found guilty of acts against the state would be openly shamed.

The people who were brought before the *bema* were not necessarily criminals. The courts that tried local murderers, thieves and other law breakers were located in a different part of the *agora*. *Bema* judgments were about loyalty to Rome. So, while the courts judged what people *did*, the *bema* judged who people *were*.

The short pillar in front of the *bema* was used as a punishment tool. After a judgment was pronounced, the guilty person was chained to this pillar, stripped of his clothing and beaten with rods, which was exactly what happened to the Apostle Paul and Silas, his co-worker, here in Philippi.

After being falsely accused of disturbing the peace and promoting practices contrary to Rome, they were abused and shamed in public, for all to see (Acts 16:19-23,37).

Later in his ministry, Paul used the image of this *bema* judgment in his letter of encouragement to the Corinthians. All believers should have a godly ambition to please the Lord, said Paul. For at his coming, we all must appear before the *bema* of Christ (2 Cor 5:10).

The Generals

They seized Paul and Silas and dragged them...before the rulers. And when they had brought them to the **magistrates**, they said, "These men are disturbing our city... " **Acts 16:19–20**

❧❧❧

Magistrates: (STRATEGOS' στρατηγός) *n.*
generals, Roman military administrators

Generals Were Generals, Not Bureaucrats

When Paul and Silas were dragged into the *agora* to be tried by the authorities, they were actually taken two places. First, their accusers took them before "the rulers." These were the local city judges. Then, they brought them to a second place, to the office of "the magistrates" (Acts 16:19-20). These men were Roman generals.

Like most conquerors, the Romans governed their provinces in two ways. In the capital cities of each province they established political administrations governed by resident proconsuls. In Macedonia's case, the proconsul lived in the city of Thessalonica and reported directly to the Roman Senate.

In other places, the military ruled. The officers of these military administrations were the Praetorians, soldiers who had been specially trained to guard the Emperor. Because they were chiefs of garrisons, the Greeks called them *strategoi* (generals). This is where the English term *strategy* comes from, for while the troops carry out the tactical plans, it's the generals who *strategize.*

These generals were not *magistrates*, the civil authorities of those days, as many English translations call them. They were military men. Since Philippi was a Roman colony, generals governed the town and its surrounding countryside.

Archaeologists believe that they have located the generals' council room at one end of Philippi's *agora*. It was a room designed much like a small theater in the round with three rectangular levels. While the accused stood down on the lowest level, the generals sat around him on higher levels. This is where the questioning, discussion and judgments took place.

How do we know that this room was the generals' office? Outside, lying on the ground, archaeologists found a triangular stone pediment which once spanned the entrance to this council room. A shield and a spear, the two well-known symbols of 1st century Roman military authorities, were carved into the front of it.

Paul's Prison

And when they had laid many stripes on them, they threw them into **prison**, charging the jailor to keep them securely, who, having received such a charge, put them into the inner **prison** and fastened their feet in the stocks. **Acts 16:23–24**

ֿ ❧❧❧

Prison: (PHULAKE′ φυλακή) *n.*
a hold, cage, guarded place

This Jail Isn't Where You Think It Is

After Paul and Silas were beaten and publicly shamed, they were thrown into prison, under maximum security, with their feet in stocks.

But where was this prison located? No one knows for sure.

Not far from the *agora*, on a hill across from the generals' office, archaeologists have found an underground vault. Since the 8th century, tradition has claimed that this is the place of Paul's imprisonment. And still today, religious pilgrims travel from faraway places to come here to stand at this spot to remember Paul's suffering.

But recent research has brought to light facts that prove that this chamber cannot have been Paul's prison. First of all, it is located in an area where four pagan temples stood at the time of the Apostle Paul. There is no logical reason why a military prison would have been located in the middle of religious sanctuaries.

Second, experts have determined that the plaster which coats the inside walls of this chamber is a type of ancient hydraulic plaster, the kind of material that in those days was only used to line the insides of water tanks. This discovery has led archaeologists to conclude that this structure was a cistern for one of the cult temples and not a prison.

So, if this water cistern (see page 35) isn't Paul's prison, where is it? We don't know. It might be located in a part of the site that has not yet been excavated, possibly behind the generals' office on the outside of the *agora*. But there's another explanation.

Many prisons from this time period that have been found in other parts of the Mediterranean have had prisoners' cells on the first floor and housing for the jailor and his family above. And these prisons were often attached to or located near the offices of the generals.

This explanation closely fits Luke's description of the events of Acts 16:23-34. In these verses, the jailor's house seems to be located close by, possibly upstairs, since he arrives on the scene quickly, and takes Paul and Silas "up" into his house (Acts 16:34 Greek).

But until further excavations take place, only the Lord knows.

The Spirit of Python

Now as we were going to the place of prayer, a slave girl who had a spirit of **divination**, met us. She brought great profit to her masters by fortune-telling. She followed after Paul and us, crying out, saying, "These men are servants of the Most High God, who proclaim to you **the** way of salvation."

Acts 16:16

❧❧❧

Divination: (PY'THON Πύθων) *n.*
the great snake who gave Apollo predicting skills

The Slave Girl and Apollo's Snake

Adjacent to the *agora*, not far from where the ancient meat market was once located, stands a lone pedestal erected in Roman times to honor a city benefactor named Pontus.

Among his many titles, which are all inscribed on this pillar, is the word *Pythonius*, which literally means, "a person of *Python*." In those days, a *Pythonius* was a person who practiced ecstatic prediction, an activity that was related to the Oracle at Delphi.

As we'll discover when we visit the temple of Apollo in Delphi, for a thousand years, female priestesses of the temple, who were known as *pythia*, while under ecstatic trances, gave special predictions called "oracles" to the petitioners who came to them seeking advice. Both *Pythonius* and *pythia* derive their names from *Python*, a mythical snake that guarded the Oracle at Delphi until it was slain by the god Apollo.

Not only does the practice of *ecstasy* connect the Oracle in Delphi with Pontus, it also connects the Oracle with the slave girl in Philippi, who in Acts 16:16 was possessed by "the spirit of divination" (literally, the spirit of *Python* in Greek) enabling her to tell fortunes for money. This activity brought great gain to her owners.

According to most English Bibles, this slave girl met Paul and his party as they were going to the place of prayer. She then followed them for days crying out, "These men are servants of the Most High God, who proclaim to you *the* way of salvation." If what she was saying was true, why did Paul get so upset with her (Acts 16:18)?

The answer can be found in the Greek text. There, in the original language, the definite article (*the*) is missing before the word *way* in her declaration. This means that the possessed girl was actually saying that Paul was preaching "*a* way of salvation," one way among many ways, not "*the* way of salvation."

This may be the reason why Paul became very annoyed, turned to the spirit and in the name of Jesus Christ cast it out of her.

The Imperial Cult

If you confess with your mouth, "Jesus is **Lord**," and believe in your heart that God raised him from the dead, you will be saved. **Romans 10:9**

ℰ ℰ ℰ

Lord: (KY'RIOS κύριος) *n.*
master, the one who has power and authority

Could You Say, Jesus is Lord?

In another part of the *agora*, across the square from the office of the generals, is the temple of the imperial cult. Local people once came to this place to worship the Emperor.

In New Testament times, an idea which Alexander the Great had introduced centuries earlier came to fruition. Alexander believed that it was a wise king who would strive to create a super culture by taking the best parts of other cultures and merging them together. So, over the next 13 years, this is exactly what he did. This practice became known as syncretism.

Religious syncretism, the practice of collecting deities from many cultures (the more the better), was a major element of Greco-Roman culture. In those days, Egyptian deities could be found in Athens and Greek gods could be found in Rome.

This was a time when pantheons (*pan* all, *theos* god) were built in many cities to house the collections of these gods. Individuals were free to create their own sets for their homes. Blessed were those who had the largest clusters for worship and protection.

Alexander went further still when he became the first Greek king who accepted worship himself. Then, the Roman Emperors who came after him not only accepted worship, they demanded it, and when this happened, the imperial cult (Emperor worship) was born.

And though people were free to worship their own assortments of gods, the worship of the Emperor was a must. Anyone who failed to do so would immediately be accused of being an enemy of the state.

Inside the temple of the imperial cult in Philippi stood a pedestal with the statue of the Emperor on top of it. In front of the statue was an altar on which a fire burned. Worshippers would enter the temple, throw incense on the fire, bow to the statue and say, "Caesar is Lord!"

In the years that followed Paul's visit to Philippi, this became a serious test for all believers, those whose only Lord was Jesus Christ. Would they dare to publicly declare, "Jesus is Lord!" or not?

The Octagon Church

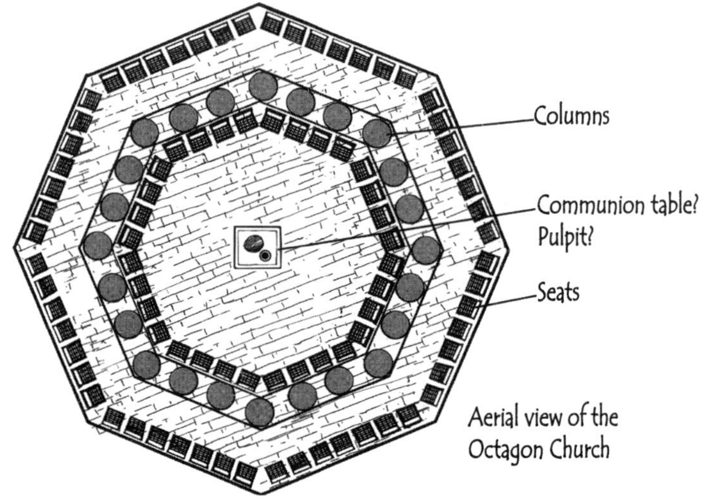

For we do not proclaim ourselves, but Jesus Christ as Lord, and ourselves as your **servants** for Jesus' sake. **2 Corinthians 4:5**

❧ ❧ ❧

Servants: (DOU'LOS δοῦλος) *n.*
slaves, those who are owned by and serve others

Brave Believers and Servant Pastors

In AD 64, fourteen years after Paul first brought the gospel of Christ to Philippi, a persecution of Christians broke out under Emperor Nero which spread throughout the Empire. It continued, with greater or lesser severity, for nearly 300 years. During these difficult times, the Christians living in Philippi became an underground community.

Then, in AD 313, the storm ended when Constantine granted the Christians religious freedom. Immediately, a group of brave believers in Philippi built a meeting place near the *agora* in the center of town, saying to their fellow citizens, "Here we are!" without any assurance that the injustices they had recently suffered would not return. This "octagon church" was the oldest building yet discovered in Europe that was originally designed to house a Christian gathering (page 35).

Unlike today's churches, the octagon church was a building in the round. Instead of sitting in a rectangular room in rows facing forward, believers took seats that were placed along the outside walls facing in. This arrangement allowed them to see in each other's faces the face of Jesus Christ as they shared communion or listened to preaching from a small platform in the center of the room, emphatically demonstrating the equal value of the many different parts of the body of Christ.

To allow the body in Philippi to function properly and to serve the needs of the members, church leaders did not assume positions of authority. Rather, they humbled themselves and became "slaves (*doulos* in Greek) for Jesus' sake" (2 Cor 4:5). By doing this, these servant pastors created a church that by the middle of the 4th century was independent, free and thriving. But such a blessed situation would be short-lived.

In AD 392, everything changed when Theodosius became Emperor and made Christianity the religion of the state. By edict, church leaders everywhere became a ruling class as Christian churches were forced to adopt the tops-down, pyramidal administrative structure of the Roman government. Instead of being free to answer to Christ, churches came under the direct control of the state. This was not a good thing.

Thessalonica

For even in **Thessalonica** you sent something more than once for my need. **Philippians 4:16**

⁂

When Paul and Silas left Philippi, their next stop was Thessalonica, which is also the next stop on our tour. Because much of this ancient city has not been excavated, we will focus our attention on one visible part of the *agora*, and after that, visit the Archaeological Museum, where we will discover some precious artifacts.

Via Egnatia—A Paved Roman Highway

Historical Center of Thessalonica

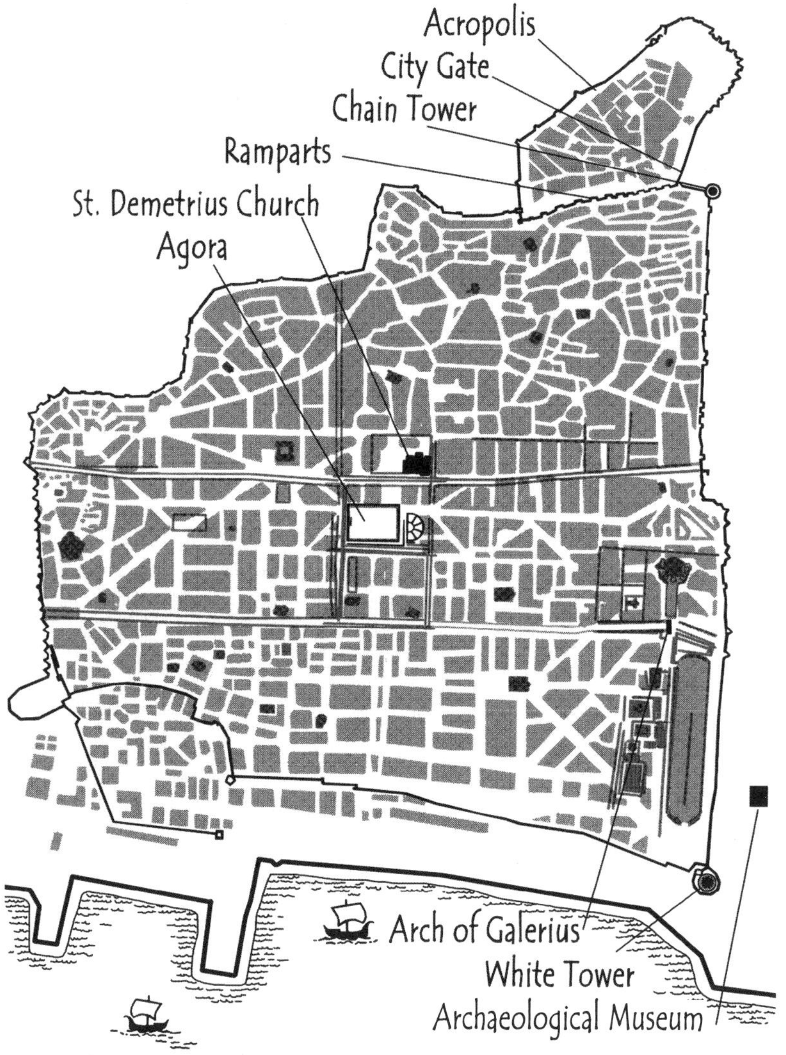

Via Egnatia

Having **passed (by)** Amphipolis and Apollonia, Paul and Silas came to Thessalonica. **Acts 17:1**

❧❧❧

Passed by: (DIODEU'O διοδεύω) *v.*
walking by a place

The Gospel Highway to the West

After preaching the gospel in Philippi and establishing a church there, Paul and Silas left their co-workers Timothy and Luke behind and departed for the next stop on their missionary journey, Thessalonica. Their route took them by Amphipolis and Apollonia as they walked along a Roman highway known as Via Egnatia (see page 62).

Near the end of the 2nd century BC, a Roman proconsul by the name of Gaius Egnatius received an order from the Roman Senate to undertake a massive project—to build a military highway all the way across Macedonia and through parts of other nearby provinces. This special roadway would enable Rome to send troops to the eastern parts of the Empire in the shortest possible time and would connect Rome with the provinces.

It took Egnatius about 20 years to build this highway, a road that was 20 feet wide in places, was entirely stone paved and was nearly 700 miles long. Every 30-35 miles, a one-day's walk, the workers built way stations, rest stops manned by garrisons of soldiers to guard the road and maintenance teams to repair it.

These stations provided food and water for travelers and their mounts and had stables with fresh horses. Milestones were placed along the road at one-mile intervals to indicate distances to nearby cities.

Via Egnatia, the first major road built by the Romans outside of Italy, was an engineering masterpiece. It was designed to maintain a constant elevation across the miles so that soldiers and equipment would not have to climb hills. To ensure that the roadbed remained solid and stable, builders dug foundations up to 15 feet deep.

Though Via Egnatia was constructed for military purposes, it also provided safety for travelers and soon became the primary commercial artery for the region. This greatly facilitated travel and communication, which supercharged the spreading of the gospel west.

The Politarchs

But the Jews, moved by envy, recruited certain wicked men of the marketplace (*agora*) and, forming a mob...dragged Jason and some fellow believers before the **city authorities.** **Acts 17:5–6**

∽∽∽

City authorities: (POLITAR'CHES πολιτάρχης) *n.*
city (*polis*) authorities (*arches*)

How Luke Documented History

Compared with the modest *agora* Paul frequented in Philippi, the city center he encountered in Thessalonica, the provincial capital, was both massive and opulent. Not only was it completely paved with marble, it took over 200 pillars to support the roof of the porch that surrounded it on all four sides.

Unfortunately, just a small part of this *agora* survives today. The rest is buried beneath the modern city's streets and buildings. What has been excavated is a piece of the ancient city's administrative section, which, though it now resembles a small theater, was once actually the site of the council chamber of the city authorities.

Luke mentions this place in Acts 17 when he describes a riot that broke out in Thessalonica as a result of Paul's preaching. When a mob that was stirred up by jealous Jews went looking for Paul but couldn't find him, they dragged his host Jason and some fellow believers into this *agora* before the city authorities at this very spot.

Instead of using other Greek words for these local officials, Luke called them *politarches*, a unique word for city (*polis*) authorities (*arches*).

Not only does this title appear nowhere else in the Bible, but through the mid-1800's, the word *politarch* was not found anywhere in Greek literature, historical records or archaeological inscriptions.

This gave liberal Bible critics an opportunity to suggest that Luke had made a serious historical error, and, based on this allegation, to claim that the Bible was inaccurate and unreliable.

In 1867, when the Ottomans who then occupied Thessalonica demolished the Royal Gate of the city, they found an inscription that contained the names of six "*politarchs*" on one of the marble stones of the foundation. This stone is now in the British Museum. Since then, archaeologists have found the word *politarch* on many inscriptions, not only in Thessalonica but in other parts of the ancient Greek world.

This discovery vindicated Luke and his New Testament writings, proving that he had "carefully investigated everything" (Luke 1:3).

The Diadem

Then I saw heaven opened, and behold, a white horse! The one riding it is called Faithful and True, and with justice he judges and makes war. His eyes are like a flame of fire, and on his head are many **diadems.** **Revelation 19:11–12**

❧❧❧

Diadem: (DIAD'EMA διάδημα) *n.*
a cloth ribbon tied around the head

A Cloth Headband—Not a Royal Crown

From the council chamber of the *politarchs* in the *agora*, we head over to the Archaeological Museum of Thessalonica which houses a treasury of artifacts from the ancient world. Many of these treasures appear in the New Testament.

One of them is the *diadem*. A *diadem* was a cloth headband that played an important role in the Greek athletic life. In those days, the ancients believed that the human body was precious because it was both the residence of the soul and a gift from the gods. So, as their way of thanking the gods for their bodies, the Greeks organized athletic competitions where the athletes could offer their victories back to the gods.

Thus, these games became part of the festivals held at local religious sanctuaries. At these gatherings, after all the sacrifices, worship and rituals had ended, the athletic competitions began. Among other things, the events included running, wrestling, boxing and chariot races.

After an athlete won an event, his trainer or the judge of the games entered the stadium and tied a cloth ribbon around his head to identify him as the victor. In Greek, this red or blue wool ribbon was called a *diadem*, a word that came from the verb *diademo*, "to bind around."

Winners of multiple events received many *diadem*s that were also wrapped around their heads. Some of these athletes, to show off their victories, would tie them around their arms or legs, wearing them proudly until the games ended.

The word *diadem* is used in the New Testament three times, (Rev 12:3; 13:1; 19:12). But each time, it is wrongly translated as a "crown" in English. *Diadems* were ribbons of victory, not royal crowns.

In Rev 19:12, John sees heaven opened and the Son of Man coming in judgment, riding a white horse. His eyes are like a flame of fire and tied around his head are many *diadem*s (not crowns), a display of the many victories this divine Conqueror has won.

The Stephanos

Do you not know that all who run in the stadium compete but only one receives the prize… They do it to receive a perishable **wreath.** **1 Corinthians 9:24–25**

∾∾∾

Wreath: (STEPH'ANOS στέφανος) *n.*
a woven head piece of ivy, oak, olive, etc.

A Perishable Wreath—Not a Royal Crown

In antiquity, in addition to the athletic competitions which took place at local temples for local people, four religious sanctuaries organized national games that were open to all Greeks. The most famous of these inter-Greek games were held in Olympia and became known as the Olympic games. Next in importance were the Isthmian games in Corinth. Then came the games at Delphi and the games of Nemea.

At the end of these national events, on the last day of competition, all of the winners, wearing their *diadems* and holding palm branches (a symbol of victory), walked in a procession to the temple sanctuary of the games' sponsoring god. There, the priests placed wreaths woven from branches (*stephanos*) on their heads as their prizes, making this special headpiece both an athletic reward and a religious symbol.

Since each of the ancient Greek gods had a favorite plant—ivy for Dionysus; myrtle for Aphrodite; for Zeus, oak or wild olive—these "perishable wreaths" (1 Cor 9:25) were made from the plant of the god who was worshipped at that particular sanctuary.

Great prestige came to the winners of these national games. Being rewarded with a *stephanos* was regarded as the supreme earthly fortune. Victory parades and celebrations broke out in the victors' cities as the towns people honored their hometown heroes.

Over time, the wearing of woven headpieces became a popular thing to do. Common people who wanted to identify themselves as members of the cult of a certain god began making their own *stephanos* out of their god's chosen plant. Temple priests also donned their wreaths during sacrifices, offerings, or other religious activities.

Since the games were still being held during Paul's lifetime, the Apostle was very familiar with the meaning of the *stephanos*. In his first letter to the Corinthians, he introduces it to us, using specific athletic terminology (1 Cor 9:24-25), as a metaphor for the reward believers will receive for successfully running the race of our Christian lives.

The Imperishable Wreath

Do you not know that all who run in the stadium compete but only one receives the prize... They do it to receive a perishable wreath, but we for an **imperishable** one. **1 Corinthians 9:24–25**

❧❧❧

Imperishable: (APH'THARTOS ἄφθαρτος) *adj.*
incorruptible, immortal, eternal, unable to decay

The King-Priest's Golden Replica

Another priceless artifact that is found in the Archaeological Museum is the imperishable wreath, a *stephanos* made of gold. Though it may look like a crown, it functioned in a very different way.

It may surprise you to learn that in the Greek New Testament, the word for a royal crown (*stemma*) is not mentioned at all. We only have ribbons (*diadem*) and wreaths (*stephanos*). The idea of a royal crown misses both the athletic and religious imagery conveyed by these words.

While the awards given at the local games had material value, the prizes of the four inter-Greek games did not. At local games, the winners received wheat, olive oil, bronze or other local products as their rewards. But the wreaths, the awards of the inter-Greek games, only carried symbolic value. The real prizes were the prestige and glory that were bestowed on the winner by his community when he went home.

Sometimes, *diadem* winners were nobles or members of royal families. These people often decorated their cloth head ribbons with gold or silver. Over time, *diadem*s became a kind of head jewelry worn publicly to distinguish the wearers as former victors in the games.

Likewise, king-priests or other priestly members of the ruling class created "imperishable wreaths," golden replicas of *stephanos*. They wore these to honor their patron god. Back then, if you saw someone wearing a golden wreath, he was probably a royal family member.

Both Paul and John mention golden wreaths in their writings. In 1 Cor 9:25, Paul says that, in contrast to the perishable wreaths given at the games, the *stephanos* the believers will receive from the Lord will be an "imperishable wreath." Not only will this reward be everlasting, it will also identify Christ-followers as members of a royal priesthood under the patronship of the real God (1 Pet 2:9).

In Rev 14:4, the Apostle John uses this same term to describe the Son of Man. Here, Christ wears an "imperishable wreath" (*stephanos*) to signify that he is God's eternal king-priest carrying out his divine, priestly administration.

Berea

And the brothers immediately sent Paul and Silas off by night to **Berea**. **Acts 17:10**

ᘓᘓᘓ

When a riot, fueled by jealous Jews, broke out against Paul and Silas in Thessalonica, the local brothers sent them off to the nearby town of Berea (today's Veria) for their own protection. During our brief stop in this town, after discussing the history of Jewish synagogues, we will visit a synagogue in the area of the one visited by Paul in Acts 17.

The Synagogue

When they got there, they went to the **synagogue** of the Jews.
Acts 17:10

❧❧❧

Synagogue: (SYNAGOGE' συναγωγή) *n.*
a Jewish meeting place, an assembly

The Origin of Synagogues

Acts 17:10 says that when Paul and Silas arrived in Berea, they went to "the synagogue of the Jews." What was a *synagogue*? The word is a Greek term that literally means "a bringing together" (*syn* together, *agō* to bring), as a collection of things, or a gathering of persons.

The Jewish synagogue that is found in the New Testament was a Jewish institution that first appeared during the Babylonian captivity. It may have started on the banks of the Tigris and Euphrates rivers by groups of Israelites who, for the first time in their history as a nation, found themselves outside of their land, enslaved by the "impure" Gentiles, with no temple or religious life. There they would gather to weep about the lost glory of Israel (Psalm 137).

Because of these circumstances, faithful Jews began to meet on a regular basis outside of the cities near river or seashores. There they could take purification baths in "living water" and encourage one another by reading the Prophets.

When the Jews returned to Jerusalem under Nehemiah and Ezra, they brought this practice with them. Even after the temple was rebuilt, synagogues functioned in parallel with it, for while there was only one temple in Jerusalem, scattered Jews gathered in synagogues in many places. When the rebuilt temple was destroyed, these meeting places became the only centers of the religious and political lives of Jewish communities. They also became places for teaching and learning.

Through the 2nd century BC, the Jews continued their custom of building synagogues outside the city walls. It was not that the Gentiles shunned them, but the Jews wanted to maintain their purity by gathering away from the cities near rivers (or seashores).

Over time, as the Jews became less religious and more secular, they began to move their synagogues inside the cities, close to the city center, to elevate their social status and increase their political power. This was especially true in large cities like Thessalonica, Athens and Corinth and is why Paul found the synagogues in these places near the *agora*.

The Scroll

And (Jesus) stood up to read. And the **scroll** of the prophet Isaiah was given to him. **Luke 4:16–17**

❧❧❧

Scroll: (BIBLI'ON βιβλίον) *n.*
a roll of parchment or papyrus for writing

Paul Was Here!

Berea's Jewish synagogue is located in a restored Jewish Quarter called Barbuta outside the city walls on a cliff overlooking a river.

This location brings to mind two words—piety and antiquity. Piety, because the synagogue is near a river where ceremonial cleansing could take place, and antiquity, since Jewish communities began to relocate inside the city walls in the 2nd century BC.

This suggests that the original synagogue in Berea—the one the Apostle Paul visited—was probably built on this site.

But there is another indication as well. Thirteen ancient scrolls were kept in this synagogue until 1943. According to Jewish scholars, one of them dated back to the 2nd century BC.

Along the margin of this special scroll, someone had handwritten a series of notes. One of the notes said that when so and so was ruling the city, a brother by the name of Saul came from Jerusalem, visited our synagogue and spoke to us about the resurrected Messiah.

In 1943, when the Nazi army invaded this place, they plundered the synagogue, taking away everything of value. Fortunately, they did not destroy the building as they had done in Thessalonica. But they did take these scrolls, including this special one, to Auschwitz, Poland where they put them in building called the Hebrew Museum.

After the collapse of Nazi Germany, the few Berean Jews who had survived demanded that this museum return these scrolls to them, including this special scroll. Instead, the museum gave this scroll to a group of Hungarian Jews, who then sold it to a Jewish art collector who now lives in Canada. Though Jewish representatives have made numerous attempts to retrieve the scroll or to at least borrow it for research purposes, the collector has refused to cooperate.

If the inscription on the scroll is authentic, it would be extremely important to Christians because it would be a historical document that would validate Paul's existence and his visit and, thereby, would further vindicate the truth of the New Testament.

Vergina

But no one in heaven or on earth or **under the earth** was able to open the scroll or look into it. **Revelation 5:3**

ኈ ኈ ኈ

From Berea, Paul traveled 200 miles south to Athens, the intellectual capital of the world. But before we follow him there, our tour now takes a detour to three non-biblical sites to discover unique ways in which Greek culture shows up in the New Testament. Our first stop is Vergina, a UNESCO World Heritage Site, where we will explore Greek ideas of the underworld by visiting underground tombs.

The Underworld

The poor man died and he was carried by the angels to Abraham's side. The rich man also died and was buried. And being in torment in **Hades**, he lifted his eyes and saw Abraham from afar and Lazarus at his side. **Luke 16:22–23**

ঌঌঌ

Hades: (HA'DES 'ᾅδης) *n.*
the Greek god of the underworld and his kingdom

Hades—The Home of the Dead

The artificial hill that you see when you enter the site at Vergina is actually a burial mound from the 4th century BC. When the mound was excavated in 1977, Professor Andronikos and his team discovered a number of royal graves, including the tomb of Phillip II, the father of Alexander the Great. Now restored as an underground museum, Vergina's tombs are one of the most important archealogical finds in history.

Though the Romans worshipped their Emperors like gods, the Greeks knew that their kings were mortals. For this reason, Phillip was entombed near the local cemetery not far from the resting places of the other mortals. His tomb was built entirely underground so that Philip would be closer to the underworld. As a king-priest, his burial chamber was designed in the shape of a small temple.

The Greeks believed that Hades was the god of the underworld, and that his domain, also called Hades, was the residence of the dead. Because they believed in life after death, the Greeks stocked their graves with the goods the departed would need for their journey to "the other side." The Greek poet, Homer, described a trip to this shadowy realm in his epic poem, The Odyssey.

According to Greek thought, when the soul leaves the body, it enters the underworld. There a boatman carries it across a river through the Gates of Hades to a place from which there is no return.

After passing the Gates of Hades, a person's eternal destiny will be determined by a group of judges based on the life he or she lived on earth. If they were pious and righteous, they would go to the place of rest. But if they were unrighteous or had committed hubris (arrogance), they would be taken to a place of torment.

In Luke 16:19-31, Jesus uses many of these Greek terms and afterlife concepts to tell the story of the deaths of Lazarus and the rich man. In this story, Jesus refers to both parts of Hades, saying that while Lazarus was carried by angels to the place of rest, when the rich man died, he found himself "in torment."

The Blessed State

Blessed are the poor in spirit, for theirs is the kingdom of heaven.
Blessed are those who mourn, for they will be comforted.
Blessed are the meek, for they will inherit the earth.

Matthew 5:3–5

ᘛᘛᘛ

Blessed: (MAKAR'IOS μακάριος) *adj.*
an inner state of complete serenity and joy
despite outward circumstances

To Experience the Life of the Gods

In Luke 16:22, Jesus referred to the peaceful section of Hades as "Abraham's side," but to the ancient Greeks, it was known as the Elysian Fields, "the isles of the blessed."

There, the righteous dead found their final home, a place where they would experience an afterlife free from toil, unaffected by life's circumstances and characterized by feelings of serenity and joy.

The term that the Greeks used to describe this blessed state was *makarios*, an untranslatable word that had a very specific meaning. The word was primarily used in connection with the gods who lived on Mount Olympus, far above the din of mortal life below. There, they enjoyed a deep tranquility that living mortals couldn't touch.

When scholars translated the Old Testament into Greek 250 years before Christ, they chose the word *makarios*, especially in the Psalms, to describe people who enjoy the favor of the God of Israel. In fact, this word opens the entire book of Psalms: "*Makarios* is the man who walks not in the counsel of the wicked..." (Psalm 1:1).

Shortly after his public ministry began, Jesus applied the idea of *makarios* to common, everyday people as he spoke of his kingdom in his famous Sermon on the Mount. "Blessed (*makarios*) are the poor in spirit," the Greek text says," for theirs is the kingdom of heaven" (Matt 5:3). Then, in this "Beatitudes" section of his sermon, as if to make a point, Jesus repeated this word eight more times.

Jesus used *makarios* in the present tense (are) to suggest that people don't have to wait until they die to enjoy "the life of the gods," but by believing in Christ, anyone can experience the blessed life of the true God right now, here on earth (John 3:16).

Later Peter, Paul and James will follow Jesus' lead, invoking the word *makarios* when they speak of our *blessed* God (1 Pet 1:3), our *blessed* hope (Titus 2:13) and the *blessed* life Christians can enjoy both now and in eternity (James 1:12).

The Divine Nature

His divine power has freely given to us everything we need for a life of godliness… he has freely given to us his precious and splendid promises, so that through them you may escape the corruption that is in the world caused by sinful desire and become **partakers of the divine nature.** **2 Peter 1:3–4**

❧❧❧

Partaker: (KOINONOS' κοινωνός) *n.*
a sharer, participant

To Share the Nature of the Gods

The ancient Greek religion was established on three very important concepts: 1) *Anthropomorphism*—attributing human shape to the gods, 2) *Theogamy*—the marriage between a god and a mortal and 3) *Theosis*—the process whereby humans become divine.

The myth of Asclepius illustrates all three. Asclepius was the son of the Greek god Apollo who had appeared in human form like a handsome man (*anthropomorphism*) and had married a mortal princess by the name of Coronis (*theogomy*). Though Asclepius was born a mortal, Apollo gave him the knowledge of herbs, which he then developed to make medicine and heal people the point of raising them from the dead. This made two other gods anxious.

One god, Mother Earth, complained to Zeus, the king of the gods, that if humans don't die anymore, the weight upon her will become so unbearable she will collapse. The other god, Hades, whose nickname Pluto means "rich one," felt poorer each time Asclepius raised someone from his underworld back to life.

So, Hades went to Zeus and argued that because Asclepius was disturbing the world order, he must die. Zeus agreed, and Asclepius died, leaving behind a widow and five children.

As Asclepius entered Hades, since he had lived a pious life, the judges sent him to the Elysian Fields. And when the gods noticed that he didn't complain about dying young, they thought highly of him. So, they invited him and his family up to Mount Olympus to enjoy a banquet with them. Feasting together with the gods, he and his family became partakers of the divine nature (*theosis*).

When Christ came, these concepts of the Greek religion became the foundations of the New Testament. 1) *Anthropomorphism*—Jesus, God Himself, became a man (1 Tim 3:16), 2) *Theogamy*—his relationship with his church is likened to a bride and groom (Eph 5:25-32) and 3) *Theosis*—God has given us everything we need for a life of godliness, that we may escape the corruption of the world and partake of his divine nature (2 Peter 1:3-4).

The Gates of Hades

On this rock I will build my church, and the **gates** of Hades will not overpower it. **Matthew 16:18**

~ ~ ~

Gates: (PY'LE πύλη) *n.*
strong, secure, prison or city doors

Christians Go Up, Not Down

When Jacob learned of the death of his son Joseph, he refused to be comforted by his other children, saying to them that he shall still be mourning when he *goes down* to Sheol to meet his son (Gen 37:35).

Yet when Stephen left this world, he didn't look down like Israel's ancient patriarchs did. Instead, he *looked up*. There, he saw heaven open and Jesus standing, ready to receive him (Acts 7:56). This fulfilled the promise that Jesus gave to his disciples at the Last Supper when he told them he was going away to prepare a place for them. And then, he would come back to pick them up (John 14:3).

In Revelation, Jesus, the Messiah, is described as the One who always was, who always is and who is "the coming one" (Rev 1:8). In the original Greek, this title, "the coming one" is the participle of the present tense. So, it doesn't mean that he will come back once in the future. Rather, he is the one who continuously comes to pick up each of his own people, starting with Stephen.

So, because Christians go up, not down, the church of Christ will never pass through the gates of Hades. Our place is in heaven.

At Vergina, there is a famous wall painting of the god Hades abducting a girl named Persephone and carrying her down to the underworld. According to Peter's preaching on the day of Pentecost, when Jesus died, he descended to Hades (Acts 2:31). There, he may have visited the Old Testament saints and the pious Gentiles who were resting in the Elysian Fields, for even though they enjoyed peace and tranquility, they were still sinners who all had open cases before God because of the debt of their sin.

In other words, though they were resting in the comfortable part of Hades, Hades was still their prison. So, Jesus may have brought good news to these pious and holy "spirits in prison" (1 Peter 3:19) that they were now free. Because of his death, their debt had been paid and the gates of Hades no longer had the power to hold them.

If they believed this, heaven welcomed them.

Meteora

I will lift up my eyes to **the hills**—from whence comes my help? My help comes from the Lord. **Psalm 121:1–2** (NKJV)

ॐ ॐ ॐ

As we leave Vergina, we drive 100 miles south to the second stop on our detour, another World Heritage Site, the monasteries at Meteora. These spectacular structures, built on mountaintops during the 14th century, give us a dramatic backdrop for lessons from church history that we can apply to our Christian lives today.

The Cave Dwellers

In those days John the Baptist began his mission in the **wilderness** of Judea, proclaiming, "Repent, for the kingdom of heaven is at hand." **Matthew 3:1**

❧❧❧

Wilderness: (ER'EMOS 'έρημος) *n.*
a deserted, uninhabited, barren, lonely place

Suffering Produces Character

Monasticism was a practice that began among Christians during the 4th century AD, some 300 years after the Apostle Paul. At that time, many changes were taking place in the church. A long period of Christian persecution had just ended, believers were enjoying new-found freedoms and church membership was growing dramatically.

Yet there were some who felt that with the end of persecution, the quality of the spiritual life of the church had diminished. Like the New Testament teaches, they believed that sufferings were a necessary part of Christian life to prove the believers' authenticity, test and build their faith and force them to exercise themselves in virtue (2 Cor 4:17; 1 Pet 1:6-9). Jesus had taught us to "love your enemy" (Matt 5:4; Luke 6:27, 35) and the persecutions were the exercises for practicing this.

One of these faithful was a man named Anthony from Alexandria in Egypt. Anthony felt that because Alexandria was a large, sinful city, the church had gradually become too secular. So, he left Alexandria to seek a closer relationship with God by isolating himself, living under harsh conditions on an island in the middle of the Nile River.

It wasn't long before he found himself surrounded by a number of other Christians who wanted to follow his example. Soon, a community began to take shape with rules of behavior that members had to promise to follow. The first three rules were chastity, poverty and obedience—practices that still govern monasticism today. From this humble beginning, the first monasteries and nunneries developed.

But Anthony was still not satisfied. He noticed that though these Christians had come out of Alexandria, Alexandria had not come out of them. They had brought Alexandria along with them in their hearts.

So, Anthony left again. This time he went to the desert near Mount Sinai where, like John the Baptist, he lived in the wilderness under even more severe conditions. Others did likewise. Because the Greek word for desert is *eremos*, these "desert dwellers" would become known as *hermits*—and their caves would be called *hermitages*.

The Monks

Do not **love** the world or the things in the world. If anyone **loves** the world, the **love** of the Father is not in him. **1 John 2:15**

❧❧❧

Love: (AGAPA'O 'αγαπάω) *v.*
to exclusively choose, value, esteem and adore

Love Not the World

By the 6th century, the monastic movement had spread from the caves at Sinai through all of the Middle East and Asia Minor. It had even reached the city of Constantinople, the capital of the empire, where there were seven monastic communities.

During a trip to Constantinople, Benedictus, a church father from the western branch of the church, made contact with the monastic lifestyle he found in this eastern branch of the church and embraced it. Then, he brought monasticism west to the Catholic Church, giving birth to the oldest Catholic monastic order, the Benedictines.

By the 11th century, the isolated caves on the sides of the cliffs of Meteora began to attract the attention of hermits. Over the next 200 years, hundreds of hermits came from many places to seek refuge there, choosing to live out their pious lives in the caves.

Near the beginning of the 14th century, a very special event took place here in Greece at Meteora. In 1312, the King of Serbia, Iaonnis Uresis Palaiologos, who was about 25 years old at that time, decided to leave his throne. After transferring the monarchy to his cousin, he came to join this community and became a disciple of Athanasios, a master who had recently arrived here from Mount Athos.

Athanasios and his disciple spent the next 13 years living together in one of the caves. One day, they decided to climb to the top of the cliffs, liked what they saw and eventually built a monastery up there. This became the first of many monasteries in Meteora.

Because of the isolation and protection that these rock mountains provided, over the years, monks built another 24 monasteries in Meteora. During the Ottoman times, many were destroyed. Others fell into disrepair. Today, only six remain.

A Quiet Life

Make it your aim to lead a quiet life, to attend to your own affairs, and to **work** with your own hands as we commanded you.

1 Thessalonians 4:11

❧❧❧

Work: (ERGA'ZOMAI 'εργάζομαι) *v.*
to engage in useful activity in contrast to idleness

Work with Your Own Hands

Before being accepted into the holy community, each new monk goes through a four-year testing period, living with the others until the day when he must decide whether he wants to join the brotherhood or not.

In these four years, he will test himself, and the brothers will test him, to determine whether he fits in or not. If so, after he participates in consecration rites, this community will become his family forever.

The monks who reside in most monasteries practice a unique lifestyle. Their daily life is divided into three parts. One part is a time of isolation and concentration when they spend time by themselves in quiet prayer, study and rest.

Another part of the day involves gathering together with the other monks for a time of corporate worship and praise to God. Here, they read the Bible, chant and participate in holy communion.

But the greatest part of the monks' day is a period of labor in which they follow the teaching of the Bible by working with their hands in some fashion. In Genesis, using symbolic language, the Bible suggests that God, like a potter with clay, created human beings with his hands (Gen 2:7.) And in Psalm 8:3, the heavens are the "work of his fingers." So, the monks use their hands to make things and serve others.

What they do depends on what type of skill they have. Some are shepherds, some cultivate the land. Others do crafts, or are carpenters, or cook the food, or make clothes.

More importantly, some use their hands to create icons, paintings which serve as books for illiterate people. They also copy manuscripts, which until the 16th century was their most important work. Day after day they transferred copy after copy of Bibles, church books or classical literature from papyrus to parchment, a great contribution to culture.

To some in the young Thessalonian church, who idled their time away and meddled in others' affairs, Paul gave a command to make it their aim to *lead a quiet life*, to attend to their own affairs and to *work with their hands* to make things and serve others (1 Thes 4:11).

The Icons

He is the **image** of the invisible God. **Colossians 1:15**

❧❧❧

Image: (EICON' εἰκών) *n.*
a visual representation, a likeness

Teach the Bible to Non-Readers

If you visit one of the monasteries here in Meteora, you will see many abstract works of art. In this part of the world, these art pieces are known as *icons*, paintings that are specially designed to represent biblical and doctrinal truths.

During the 1st century, because the church was under the influence of Judaism, it did not permit the use of visual art for decoration nor allow images of any kind in the church. But by the 4th century, portraits of martyrs, heroes of the faith, began to find their way into churches.

These early paintings were never meant to be worshipped like pagan cult images but were simply intended to remind the faithful of who their brave forefathers were—much like photographs do today.

In AD 381, the Roman Emperor Theodosius made Christianity the religion of the Empire, abolished other religions and began to persecute the pagans. As a result, pagans flooded into the church and began to worship these *icons* in the same way they had worshipped their cult statues in the past. Large numbers of new "Christians" venerated these portraits and addressed their prayers to them.

This practice continued until a Byzantine Emperor named Leo III the Isaurian came into power in the 8th century. Leo realized that the church was fast becoming a pagan institution. So, he ordered the removal of all the *icons* from the churches. As you might expect, many icon worshippers reacted badly to this decision and fighting broke out. History would call this struggle, the "iconoclastic controversy."

During the 9th century, due to a worldwide shortage of book-making materials (papyrus), church leaders voted to bring *icons* back into churches, not to be worshipped as pagan idols, of course, but to become the spiritual "books" for the illiterate to read.

This decision led to the creation of the two-dimensional, abstract style of painting that is on display in the monasteries. It was used to visually deliver biblical truth—the gospel message—to non-readers.

Delphi

What advantage then has the Jew?... they were entrusted with the **oracles** of God. **Romans 3:1-2**

~~~

Before rejoining Paul in Athens, our final stop is Delphi, a special, spiritual place for Greeks. Here, at the center of the Greek world, we'll gain an understanding of the famous "Oracle of Delphi," we'll explore athletic events held at the stadium and we'll discuss three important artifacts found in the archaeological museum.
~~~

Delphi's Location

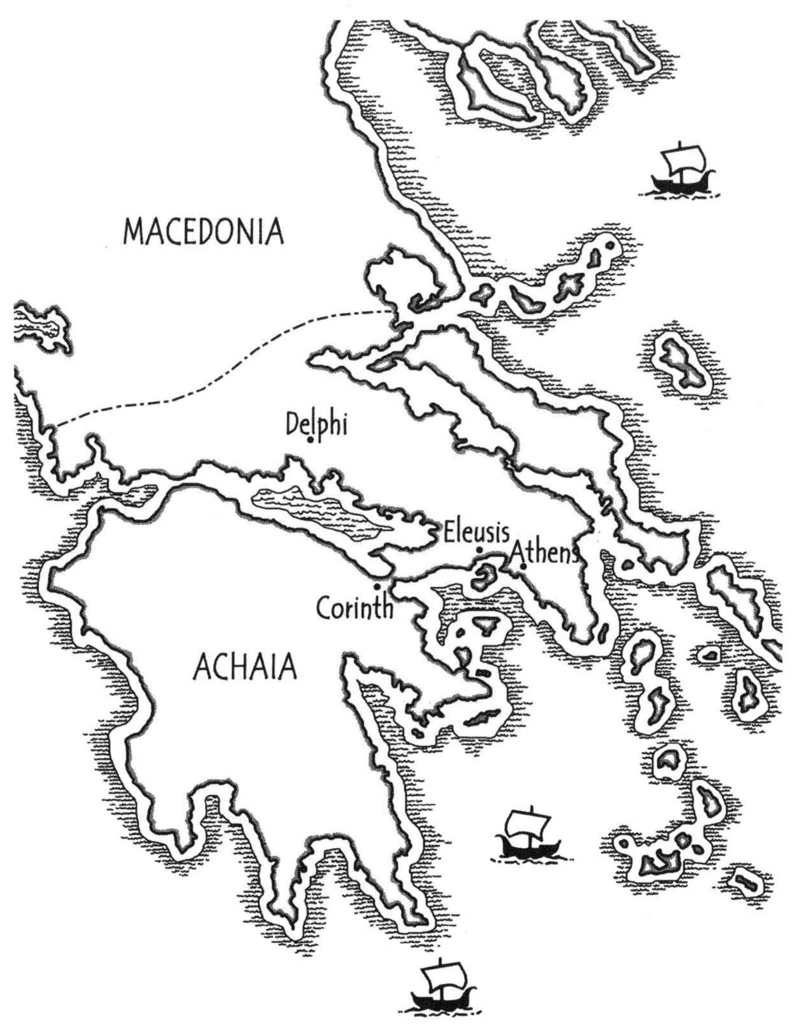

Ancient Delphi

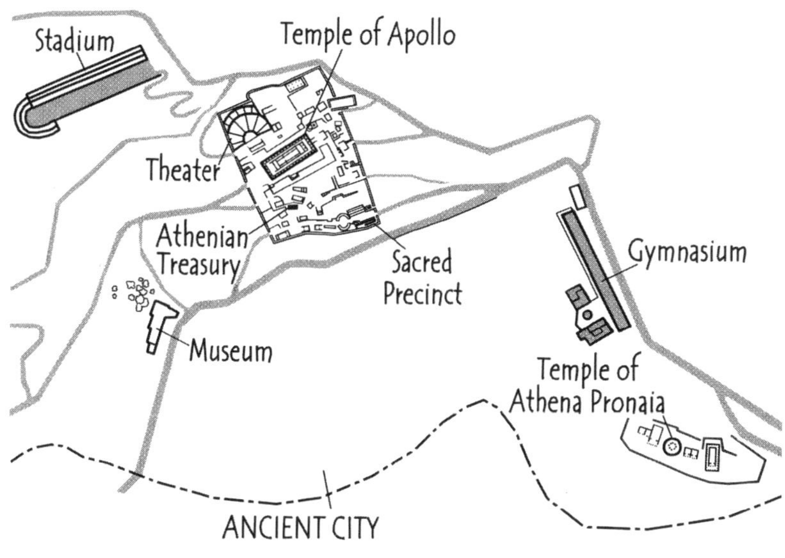

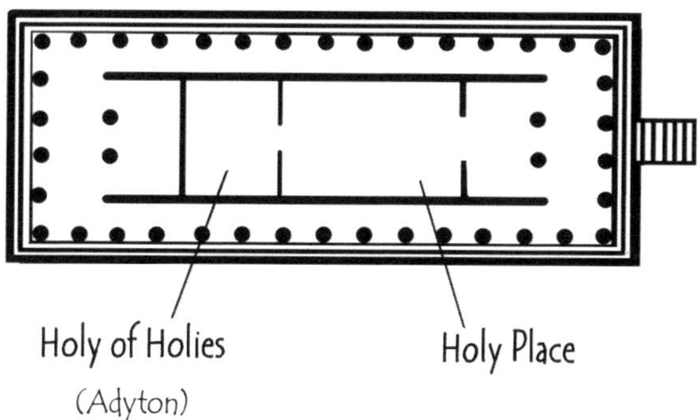

The Oracle of Delphi

Moses was **warned** by God when he was about to erect the tabernacle. **Hebrews 8:5**

❧❧❧

Warned: (CHRĒMATI'ZŌ χρηματίζω) *v.*
a divine communication or revelation

Intoxicated Goats (and Priestesses)

Before we speak about the Oracle of Delphi, we need to understand what an oracle is. To the Greeks, an oracle meant three things. First, it meant a message, a communication, a revelation from a god. Second, the oracle was the mediator, the *person* who received and delivered the message. And third, it was the *place* where the message was delivered.

All three of these oracle aspects appear in the Bible. In Exodus 19, Moses was the *person* who received *messages* directly from God and delivered them to the children of Israel. The *place* was Mount Sinai.

During the second half of the 2nd millennium BC, about the time Moses was on Mount Sinai, something was happening on a different mountain. In Delphi, on the slopes of Mount Parnassus, a group of shepherds noticed that vapors were rising up from a crack in the earth. They also noticed that when their goats inhaled these vapors, they became intoxicated.

One of the shepherds, a man named Coretas, decided to breathe these vapors himself to see what happened. Immediately, he began to scream and speak wildly. Though this terrified the others, they heard among his confused rantings clear words that revealed their personal secrets and predicted future events. This frightened them even more.

The shepherds interpreted this phenomenon as their goddess, the Mother Earth, trying to speak with them. So, they built an enclosure around the crevasse, dedicated this holy precinct to her and appointed a priestess who would receive her messages by breathing these gases. This is how the Oracle of Delphi began.

When the Dorians came to this place in the 12th century BC, they brought with them their worship of Apollo and changed this Oracle from Mother Earth's sanctuary to the place where priestesses delivered Apollo's guidance instead. Eventually the temple of Apollo was built here on the slopes of Mount Parnassus.

And for the next 1,500 years, people from all over the world came to Delphi to hear Apollo's predictions or seek his advice.

The Temple of Apollo

For a tent was set up. The outer room… was called "the **Holy** Place." Behind the curtain was a second room, a shrine called "the Most **Holy** Place." **Hebrews 9:2-3**

❧❧❧

Holy: (HAGION ἅγιον) *adj.*
separate from common; dedicated; sacred

Similar Sanctuaries

The ruins of Apollo's temple in Delphi date back to the 4th century BC. This was not a typical one-room Greek sanctuary built to house the cult statue of a special god. No. Apollo's temple was different.

Its design reminds us of the temple in Jerusalem. The two were strikingly similar in form and function. Both buildings had two rooms: an outer room, "the holy place," and an inner room called, "the holy of holies" or "the Most Holy Place" (page 103).

And just as an Old Testament high priest entered the holy of holies once a year to make atonement for the sins of the people, the priestess of Apollo, called the Pythia, entered the inner chamber of this temple only once a year on Apollo's birthday to deliver his will to the people.

As this day approached, groups from all over the world—heads of state, country delegations, people with family problems—made their way to Delphi with requests in hand for predictions or advice from Apollo. After walking part way up this mountain, they stopped, offered sacrifices and took purification baths, hoping that their petitions would be chosen by the priests and carried forward into Apollo's presence.

Those who were selected walked further up the Sacred Way to the temple of Apollo. There, three male priests (interpreters) met them, made a list of their entreaties and entered the temple with the priestess.

The priestess then proceeded into the holy of holies alone, sat on a special tripod stool and began to inhale the intoxicating vapors that ascended out of the mouth of a deep cavern beneath the floor. When she fell into a trance and began hallucinating uncontrollably, the male priests waiting outside interpreted what they heard and wrote down Apollo's will, usually in poetic form.

Apollo's temple with its priestly service and oracles may have been patterned after God's true temple. For his own reasons, to serve his own purposes, God seems to have allowed Apollo's temple with its Oracle to function credibly for centuries.

But, after Christ came, the Oracle spoke no more.

The Oracle's Predictions

For all the **prophets** and the law prophesied until John.
Matthew 11:13

Prophet: (PROPHE'TES προφήτης) *n.*
spokesperson, representative speaker

Predictions Are Not Prophecies

The Oracle of Delphi became world famous for the predictions that were made there. And in the books that were written about Delphi, this predictive phenomenon is often called *prophecy.* But I avoid using this term for one good reason: the word *prophecy* means something else.

Prophecy is a Greek word made from two other words, *(pro),* "in front of or before" and (*phemi*), "I speak." So, literally, *prophecy* means, "I speak in front of or before someone." It has more to do with announcements than with predictions.

The word *prophecy* was first used in Greece during the period of monarchy. When kings planned to visit their subjects, since they didn't have telephones, they sent *prophetes* ahead of them, official spokesmen, to preannounce their coming. And when questions arose, the *prophetes* interpreted what the king meant by what he said. This gave the people time to properly prepare for their royal visit.

This is what *prophecy* means.

In this same sense, the Old Testament prophets were God's official spokesmen, preannouncers, interpreters, sent out to speak his words in front of his people in anticipation of his arrival. Their primary purpose wasn't to make predictions about the future. They came to prepare the nation for the coming Messiah by changing peoples' hearts.

When Greek prophets were dispatched, they took special staffs with them, called *kerykeion* in Greek, bearing the king's seal as their credentials. These staffs authorized them to speak on behalf of the king.

But when God sent his prophets out, instead of giving them special staffs, he gave them a partial knowledge of the future so the people would listen to them. These predictions were their credentials.

Who was the greatest prophet? According to Jesus, it was John the Baptist (Matt 11:11-13). Yet, John never made any predictions, performed any miracles or gave any ecstatic utterances like the Sibyls.

No. John was the greatest person who ever lived because he announced the coming of the King of Kings (Matt 3:1-12).

The Sibyls

A slave girl who had a spirit of divination met us. She brought great profit to her masters by **fortune-telling**. **Acts 16:16**

❧❧❧

Fortune-telling: (MANTEUO'MAI μαντεύομαι) *v.* predicting, manic raving

Pagan Priestesses Who Predicted Christ

On the ceiling of the Sistine Chapel, surrounding nine scenes from Genesis, Michelangelo painted images of twelve people who predicted the coming of Jesus Christ. In addition to seven male Old Testament prophets, he interspersed, side by side, five female Sibyls, pagan Greek priestesses of Apollo. One was from the Oracle of Delphi.

The confirmed accuracy of the Sibylline oracles so impressed early Christian apologists and church fathers, including Augustine, that they concluded that, like the Old Testament prophets, God had given prophetic gifts to the Sibyls. Michelangelo's Prophets and Sibyls testify, then, of the continuous wait of all mankind for their Redeemer.

The Delphic Sibyl predicted Christ's coming in an oracle given to Octavius Augustus in 31 BC. In that year, Octavian defeated Mark Anthony and Cleopatra in a sea battle that took place close to Delphi. Then, Octavius faced a dilemma—should he invade Egypt to destroy the enemy, once for all, or should he return to Rome to be crowned the Emperor before battling Egypt? If he invaded Egypt first, Rome might forget him. If he returned to Rome, the enemy could rearm.

So, Octavian came to the Oracle to seek advice. The Delphic Sybil said to him: "A Jewish child ordered me to go down to Hades and to stay there in silence. This Jewish child is going to reign eternally. Therefore, go away from my sanctuaries and be in silence yourself."

The other Sibyls on Michelangelo's ceiling predicted the coming of Christ as the "Master of the Golden Age," a person who would usher in a period of world peace and harmony. One described him as a star rising from a virgin. Another said that in the Golden Age there won't be famine because the Master can feed 5,000 men with five loaves.

And another Sibyl said that since the Master can touch lepers and heal them, the coming age will be disease free. Just like the Magi were informed from above about Christ's birth, God worked with the Sibyls of the pagan world to preannounce the Messiah's coming.

The Athletic Life

Everyone who competes exercises self-control in all things... So I do not run aimlessly; I do not box like one flailing the air. But I **discipline** my body and bring it into subjection...

1 Corinthians 9:25–27

ॐ ॐ ॐ

Discipline: (HYPOPIA'ZO ὑπωπιάζω) *v.*
to hit someone under their eye with your fist

Paul the Athlete?

The long rectangular ruins found at the border of the archaeological site belong to the gymnasium (page 103), the place where the athletes prepared themselves to compete in the Pythian Games, the inter-Greek games held at Delphi. Since many competitors came from faraway places, they arrived at Delphi at least one month before the start of the games to adjust themselves to the local conditions and to complete their training programs.

The gymnasium, located at the bottom of the site, was exactly the same length as the stadium, located at the top of the site. But unlike the stadium, the gymnasium had a roof for all-weather training.

It may surprise you to learn that the athletes were completely naked when they competed in their events, a practice which dates back to the 8th century. Athletic nudity, for the Greeks, who idealized the human body, spoke to strength, discipline, freedom and virtue.

The two English words, *gymnasium* and *gymnastics* come from the same Greek word, *gymnos*, which means "naked." *Gymnasium*, then, is the place of naked men and *gymnastics*, the activity of naked men.

Jews were prohibited from participating in these games for two important reasons. First, except under special circumstances, Jews were not allowed to be seen naked in public. And second, the games had a pagan religious character that was blasphemous to them.

So, because he was a Jew, the Apostle Paul would not have been permitted to participate in these sporting events. Yet in his letters, Paul speaks like an experienced athlete who knows all about running, boxing and wrestling when he uses technical terms known only to those who have been trained in these sports.

In 1 Cor 9:27, the English phrase, "I *discipline* my body," is a very special boxing term conveyed through one Greek word. This word literally means, "I punch someone with a fist beneath their eye making it black and blue." Only an experienced boxer would know that this is the word for the hardest punch of all.

The Stadium

Therefore since we ourselves have so great a cloud of witnesses surrounding us, let us also lay aside every **impediment**, and the sin that so easily distracts, and let us run with endurance the race that is prescribed for us, fixing our gaze upon Jesus, the pioneer and perfecter of our faith. **Hebrews 12:1–2**

❧❧❧

Impediment: (OG'KOS 'όγκος) *n.*
volume, bulk, clothing

Where We All Run Naked in Public

Specific athletic terminology also appears in the letter to the Hebrews. This is quite surprising since Hebrews were not allowed to participate in the games. How is it possible, then, for the writer to send a letter to a group of Jewish Christians using illustrations taken from pagan life?

The answer is that at the time this letter was written, there were two major groups of Jews—Zealots and Hellenists. The Zealots railed against Gentile practices. But the Hellenistic Jews had adopted the Greek lifestyle so completely that a gymnasium was found in Jerusalem that dated back to the 2nd century BC.

Hebrews 12:1-2 describes an athletic event that reminds us of the stadium in Delphi. "We ourselves have so great a cloud of witnesses surrounding us." Who are these witnesses? Possibly, they are the martyrs who are described in the previous chapter of Hebrews. But they also might be God, the angels, the devil, demons—all pictured sitting in the stadium, watching the athletes running down below.

The writer continues. "Let us put down every *impediment*." But the English word *impediment* doesn't accurately convey what's really happening here. Literally, the writer says, "Let us lay aside everything that creates a *volume* on our body." Not an impediment. Not a weight. But a garment, a toga, a *volume*.

"And let us run (*naked*) with endurance the race that is prescribed for us." This is a perfect illustration of the transparency of the Christian life, a life which is not lived privately, but publicly. We are running the race of our lives *naked* in front of God and everyone else.

As the Pioneer and Perfecter of our faith, Christ perfects us in much the same way a trainer develops his athletes. In those days, most of the trainers were former athletes themselves. They had won races. They knew the best techniques. And they conveyed their knowledge, experience and encouragement to their runners.

This is Jesus in Hebrews. He ran the perfect race. He knows the best way to run. And he's training us to run our races just like he did.

The Foot Race

And let us run with endurance the race that is prescribed for us, **fixing our gaze upon** Jesus. **Hebrews 12:2**

~ ~ ~

Fix our gaze upon: (APHORA'O 'αφοράω) *v.*
to focus on earnestly and exclusively

Focus on the Post

Of all the track and field events that took place in Delphi, the sprints (*stadion* in Greek) were by far the most exciting and prestigious. These foot races were contests for individuals (never groups) which covered a distance of one *stadia* (the length of the *stadium*), a fixed interval of about 200 meters or ⅛ of a Roman mile.

Both Luke and John used the word *stadia* as a unit of measure in their New Testament books. In Luke's Gospel, the road to Emmaus ran 60 *stadia* (7 miles) from Jerusalem (Luke 24:13). In John 6:19, the disciples had rowed around 25 or 30 *stadia* (3 or 4 miles) before Jesus, walking on water, caught up with them. And John's spectacular vision of the New Jerusalem included dimensions of the city that stretched 12,000 *stadia* (1,500 miles) in all directions (Rev 21:16).

Unlike today's stadiums where runners compete on oval tracks, the ancient Greek stadiums were rectangular fields. For longer races, the athletes would run the length of the field, turn around and run back. And like horses that are separated by gates at the start of horse races, runners were separated by vertical posts placed in holes that were cut into grooved starting blocks.

Though there were no fixed lanes for the runners to follow, a second set of posts was set up at the opposite end of the field which mirrored their starting positions and gave the runners targets to run to. Runners needed skill to turn quickly around the posts and stamina for completing longer races.

At the start of each race, competitors lined up on their starting blocks and focused intently upon the posts in the distance to block out the crowd noise and eliminate distracting thoughts. Then, as they ran, they continued to stare at their posts with tunnel vision.

The writer of Hebrews chose this exciting scene to illustrate the way Christians should go about living our lives. As we run our own prescribed races, with skill and stamina, we look away from everything else, fixing our gaze upon Jesus, the post standing before us.

The Gallio Inscription

But when Gallio was **proconsul** of Achaia, the Jews rose up with one accord against Paul and brought him before the (*bema*)...

Acts 18:12

ꕥ ꕥ ꕥ

Proconsul: (ANTHY'PATOS 'ανθύπατος) *n.*
the governor of a Roman province

The Emperor's Letter to Delphi

The fragmentary inscription that you see etched in stone near the entrance of the Archaeological Museum at Delphi is one of two writings on display that survives from antiquity.

It was found in Delphi near the temple of Apollo in the early 1900's and is part of a letter sent by Emperor Claudius to introduce the new governor of Achaia. You may remember that during New Testament times, Achaia was the Roman province that occupied the southern part of Greece. Corinth was its capital.

This new governor was Gallio, a noble Roman, whose brother Seneca was a philosopher and the tutor of Nero. Gallio is mentioned in Acts 18:12 as the proconsul of Achaia who was in Corinth at the time of Paul's first visit and before whom Paul appeared in judgment.

Among other things, the inscription says that Emperor Claudius was "acclaimed Imperator for the 26th time," which dates the writing sometime in the middle of AD 52. Since proconsuls served one-year terms and usually took office on May 1st, Gallio was probably in Corinth during the last half of AD 51 and the first half of AD 52.

This fixes the date of the Apostle Paul's arraignment before Gallio in Corinth and enables more precise dating of his missionary journeys and letters. For this reason, the Gallio inscription is one of the most important discoveries in history for Christian apologetics.

> *Tiberius Claudius Caesar Augustus Germanicus... acclaimed Imperator for the twenty-sixth time... sends greetings to the city of the Delphians. For a long time, I have been well disposed toward the city of Delphi, but also solicitous for its prosperity... but now it is said to be destitute of citizens, as L. Julius Gallio, my friend and proconsul recently reported to me...*

The Charioteer

And I turned to see the voice that was speaking to me, and when I had turned I saw seven golden lampstands, and in the midst of the lampstands one like a son of man, dressed in a long robe and with a gold **sash** tied high across his chest. **Revelation 1:13**

❧❧❧

Sash: (ZO'NE ζώνη) *n.*
an encircling band, a belt

Dressed Like Apollo

If you were to visit the Stoa Museum in Athens, you would see a cult statue of Apollo that will remind you of the charioteer, the masterpiece of the Delphi museum. Discovered in 1896, "the charioteer of Delphi" is considered one of the finest examples of 5th century bronze sculpture. It was thought to have been created to commemorate a victory at the Pythian Games held at Delphi.

During a time when men were depicted totally naked, both the Stoa statue of Apollo and the charioteer of Delphi are fully clothed and are dressed the same way, in full-length garments with sashes. Why?

In Greek mythology, Apollo was the god of culture and music. As the god of culture, he is portrayed wearing the long garment of the king-priest, and as a musician, he wears a sash tied high across his chest to hold up his musical instrument.

But Apollo was also the god of light, a charioteer who rode the chariot of the sun across the sky. Ancient musicians and charioteers, who were both under Apollo's protection, often dressed like he did. This is why the charioteer of Delphi wore these clothes.

Notice one other striking feature about this chariot driver. He has a ribbon, a diadem, tied around his head, signifying that he is a victor. This reminds us of Jesus, the Victor of Victors, who in Revelation 19 appears with many diadems tied around his head (page 68).

The ancient Ions, including the people who lived in Ephesus in Asia Minor, believed that they were descendants of Apollo. For this reason, king-priests from this region dressed like Apollo, wearing long, sashed garments.

At the time when the Apostle John wrote the book of Revelation from Patmos, he was living in Ionia. This may be why in Rev 1:13, Jesus appeared to John dressed in the full-length garment of the Ionian kings, communicating that he is coming back, not as a barefoot teacher walking among the people of Galilee, but as the real Apollo, the victorious, conquering King-Priest.

Athens

Those who conducted Paul brought him as far as **Athens**, and receiving an order for Silas and Timothy to come to him as soon as possible, they left. **Acts 17:15**

❧❧❧

From Delphi, we head to Athens to rejoin Paul on his missionary journey through Macedonia and Achaia. In our tour of this important destination, we will talk about the city's namesake, Athena, follow Paul's movements during his visit and discover how the concepts of Athenian democracy and Greek philosophy enriched the language and meaning of the New Testament.

Athens' Location

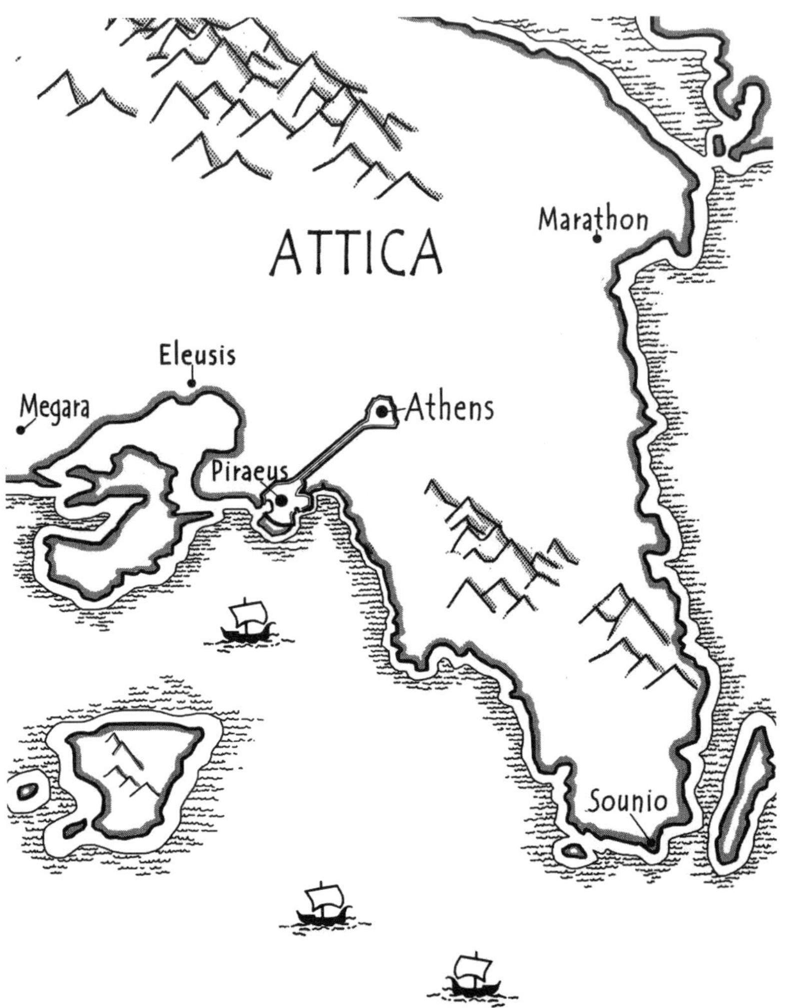

Ancient Athens

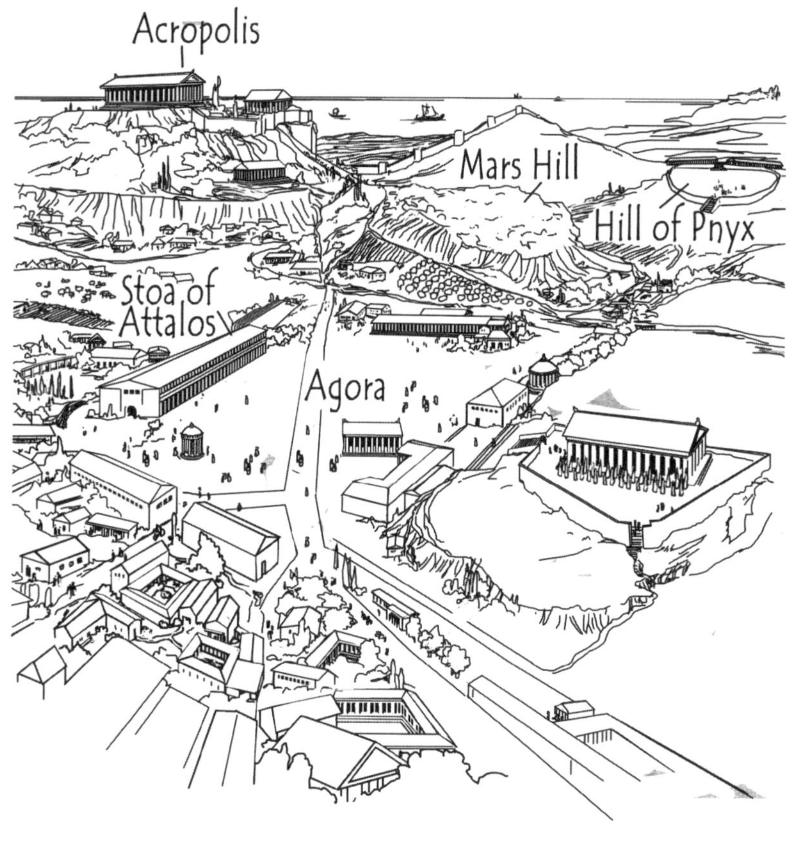

Athena

Does not wisdom cry out? And understanding lift up her voice? She takes her stand on the top of the high hill. Beside the way, where the paths meet. She cries out by the gates, at the entry to the city, at the entrance of the doors... I, wisdom, dwell with prudence, and find out knowledge and discretion... By me kings reign, and rulers decree justice... I love those who love me, and those who seek me diligently will find me. Riches and honor are with me, enduring riches and righteousness

Proverbs 8:1-21 (NKJV)

❧❧❧

Wisdom: (SOPHI'A σοφία) *n.*
superior insight, learning and knowledge used positively

Lady Wisdom

I would like to begin our conversation about Athens on the Acropolis at the Parthenon, a temple dedicated to Athena, Lady Wisdom, the patron goddess of the Athenians.

This massive marble temple, which measured 230 feet long, 100 feet wide and 45 feet high, was built with 16,500 uniquely-designed pieces in only nine years. The Parthenon housed an equally immense gold and ivory statue of the goddess, which was itself nearly 40 feet tall. For over a thousand years, Lady Wisdom stood in her sanctuary high above Athens, overlooking her beloved city.

But before we say more about *this* Lady Wisdom, I would like to remind you of *another* Lady Wisdom found in your Bibles in the book of Proverbs, especially in chapter eight. There, this biblical "person" called "Wisdom" describes herself in great detail and itemizes the gifts she brings to the people who love her (Prov 8:1-21).

She possesses knowledge and discretion, hates pride, arrogance and evil behavior and knows how to govern righteously. She calls out to all mankind with words of truth and knowledge, urging people everywhere to choose her over silver, gold or rubies.

What is striking about this is that during the 5th-4th centuries BC, (the Classical Period) the Athenians received all the gifts of Wisdom mentioned in Proverbs—the glory, riches, knowledge, prudence in governing—and changed the history of the world, in spite of the fact that Athens was a very small place. Why was Athens so blessed?

It might be because the Athenian people chose to honor wisdom instead of the worship of Aphrodite, Zeus or any of the other ancient gods. Their constant pursuit of wisdom turned these people into *philosophers* (friends of wisdom) and led some of them to discover the one true God. In time, God would use these wise Greeks to prepare the minds of the world's people to receive his Son, Jesus Christ, the Wisdom of God (1 Cor 1:24).

Athena's Birth

In the beginning was the Word, and the Word was **with** God, and the Word was God. **John 1:1**

ঌ ঌ ঌ

With: (PROS' πρός) *prep.*
facing, moving towards

A Picture of Christ

When the Athenians built the Parthenon and dedicated it to the goddess Athena, the daughter of Zeus, they depicted her birth on the eastern pediment of the building in a unique and extraordinary way.

According to an ancient myth, one day, Zeus had a terrible headache and asked Hephaestus, the god of blacksmiths, to help him. Hephaestus "helped" Zeus by splitting his head open with his axe, and out jumped Athena, not as a baby, but as a full-grown adult, armed with a shield, a spear and a helmet.

What might this story imply? First, it might suggest that wisdom often comes after many headaches. Second, that wisdom is fully developed and never arrives prematurely. And third, that wisdom is equipped and prepared to face any situation.

When the sculptor Pheidias designed this pediment, he placed Zeus, the father god, in the center, sitting on his throne. Athena is beside him, her body in motion as if she had just jumped out of his head. Yet, her face is turned towards his. This very special posture suggests that she is moving *towards* her father.

This scene reminds us of Proverbs 8:22-31 where Christ is pictured as the personified "Wisdom" of the Old Testament, established from eternity, before the Lord had created the heavens and the earth. He stands beside him, like a master workman, and was daily his delight.

This scene also brings to mind the opening of John's Gospel, in which the Word, the eternal Son of God, is the agent of creation, is positionally *with* God, moving towards him (John 1:1-3). Like the images of Zeus and Athena decorating the Parthenon, the Father and the Son are face to face.

Could it be that John is bringing the minds of his Greek readers back to this well-known decoration on the house of Lady Wisdom, intending to show them that Jesus, the Word of God, the eternal One who is at the Father's side, has come to make him known?

The Pillars

The one who conquers, I will make him a **pillar** in the temple of my God and he will never go out of it. **Revelation 3:12**

❧❧❧

Pillar: (STY'LOS στΰλος) *n.*
a post, column, standing memorial

Pillars Become People Who Become Pillars

Among the treasured artifacts found in Greece are pillars shaped like people—like the women holding up the south porch of the Erechtheion temple on the Athenian acropolis. Yet, before the 7th century BC, because the Greeks believed that their gods were spiritual beings, they never made statues of them. Instead, whenever they wanted to memorialize a god's divine presence in a place, they erected a simple stone pillar.

We find a similar practice in the Old Testament. In Genesis, after Jacob saw a vision of a heavenly ladder, he said, "Surely God is in this place." Then, he took a stone, set it up as a pillar and called the name of the place Bethel, "house of God" (Gen 28:16-19).

Later, at Moses' time, we see God leading the children of Israel through the desert in a pillar of cloud during the day and a pillar of fire at night (Exo 13:21). Once again, a pillar symbolized divine presence. This practice continued in many places until the 7th century BC.

Then, during the time of the Athenian democracy, simple human beings, who before this time had no value whatsoever, became the most valued part of society (see page 23). When this happened, for the first time in human history, the Greeks began depicting their gods in human form, each with a different human appearance.

Soon, statuary—monuments as art—emerged as an art form as sculptures of the gods with idealized human bodies began to appear in Greece. Pillars began to look like people.

This concept of the humanization of divinity spread across the world by the campaigns of Alexander the Great. Pagan peoples in many places began to think of their gods in human form. In Acts, when Paul and Barnabas visited Lystra, the Lycaonians proclaimed, "The gods have come down to us *in the likeness of men*" (Acts 14:8-18).

This helps explain why Christianity became more popular among Gentiles than among the Jews. That God would come in human form, an idea that was blasphemous for the Jews, was very easy for the nations to accept. God was preparing the world for the incarnation of Christ.

Hadrian's Breastplate

So (Paul) reasoned in the synagogue with the Jews and the worshippers, and in the **marketplace** every day with those who happened to be there. **Acts 17:17**

❧❧❧

Marketplace: (AGORA' 'αγορά) *n.*
the town square, city center, social hub

The Agora of Athens

From the Parthenon, we come down to the *agora* of Athens, the first purpose-built town square in history. This city center from the 6th century BC housed administrative offices and areas for religious, political and commercial activities. It was also the birthplace of Athenian democracy, which we will speak more about later.

Over time, the Greek noun *agora* gave birth to two Greek verbs. The first was *agoreuo*, which means, "I make speeches." During the time of the Athenian democracy, this *agora* was the place where the people made speeches. The second verb was *agorazo*, literally, "I buy." This spoke to the commercial activities of this place.

During Paul's visit to Athens, besides reasoning with the Jews in the synagogue, he wandered through the *agora* daily, speaking with those who happened to be there (Acts 17:17). This was the place where he met the philosophers who then brought him to the top of Mars Hill, where he delivered his famous speech (Acts 17:22-31).

One special artifact found in the *agora* is the statue of Hadrian, the Emperor of Rome sometime after Paul's visit to Athens. Though a Roman, Hadrian was educated in Athens and admired the Greek culture so much that he became a financial supporter of the city.

The scene carved into Hadrian's breastplate portrays two infant brothers, Romulus and Remus, drinking milk from a she-wolf. According to Roman mythology, when these brothers grew up, they founded the city of Rome and became the symbols of its people.

The breastplate also shows a woman with an owl, the emblem of wisdom, standing on top of the she-wolf. Beside her are two *Nikes*, "winged victories," crowning her. Who is she? She is Athena, Lady Wisdom, being honored. But what is the point of this imagery?

Hadrian is declaring that Athens is culturally superior to Rome and that Rome is the support upon which Greek culture must stand. As the Roman poet Horace once said, "Although we conquered Greece with our weapons, she conquered us with her culture."

The Assembly of Athens

For as in our one **body** we have many members, and the members do not all have the same function, so we who are many are one **body** in Christ, and individually members who belong to one another. **Romans 12:4–5**

❧❧❧

Body: (SOM'A σώμα) *n.*
a collective unity in community

One Body with Many Members

When we introduced the first Greek miracle, Athenian democracy, we mentioned how a nobleman named Cleisthenes had gathered ordinary citizens and formed them into the first assembly of Athens.

This group of men over 20 years old began to meet together to discuss common problems and soon became the highest governing authority of the city. For the first time in history, administrative power had shifted from the ruling class to ordinary people.

All of the important issues related to the life of the city were brought before this body, who then decided how to resolve them. Each member had the right to speak about and vote on the proposals that were brought before this united citizen group.

The assembly of Athens met in the *agora* and gathered there more than 40 times a year. Members were paid a daily wage for their participation in the meetings.

Cleisthenes was the first person in recorded history to model a group of people after the human body (*soma* in Greek). He told the assembly, "You are the living body in this place. As members of this assembly, you are the members of this body. As individuals, you have distinct personalities which make your contributions unique and necessary. So, please participate in the common life of this body."

Years later, in his letters to the Roman and Corinthian churches, the Apostle Paul would use the same terminology of this well-known element of Greek culture to describe the essential nature of the Christian community.

Speaking to these Gentile churches in their own cultural language, Paul said that, like the members of the assembly of Athens, the believers are members of the body of Christ. And though all the members of his body have equal value and status, their different giftings blend together spiritually, in Christ, to express him and carry out God's work for the betterment of society (1 Cor 12:12-20).

Insiders and Outsiders

How can anyone in the position of an **outsider** say, "Amen," to your thanksgiving since he does not know what you are saying?

1 Corinthians 14:16

And coming to find that they were uneducated and common (*idiotes*) men, they were astonished and recognized that they had been with Jesus. **Acts 4:13**

Outsider: (IDIOT'ES 'ιδιώτες) *n.*
a private, foolish, uninformed person

Citizens and Idiots

During the time of the Athenian democracy, members of the local society separated themselves into two groups: those who rushed to participate in the new system, something that they had never heard of or seen before, and the others who chose not to join the assembly.

The townspeople who involved themselves in the life of the city (*polis*) became known as citizens (*polites*). To be a citizen meant to take part in the local *political* process. That Paul was a citizen of Tarsus (Acts 21:39) suggests that he was engaged in the common life of that city.

The other Athenians, those who chose not to join the assembly, were usually the rich people who were more concerned about their own interests than the public good. They tended to live private lives outside of the system.

Since these private people did not attend the assembly meetings, they were uninformed about city matters. For this reason, the insiders called these people "outsiders" (*idiotes*), a Greek word which means *private*. Over time, the word *idiotes* took on a negative connotation. To the insiders, the outsiders were useless *idiots*.

Paul used this term when he wrote to the Corinthians about the use of spiritual practices in public worship. If "outsiders" (*idiotes*) might visit your meetings, said Paul, they would not understand what was going on (1 Cor 14:16). This word also appears in Acts chapter four, where, after healing a man lame from birth, Peter and John were jailed by the Jewish leaders. Then they questioned them (Acts 4:1-13).

When the council observed the boldness of Peter and John, both in quoting Scripture and in testifying of what God has done, they were amazed because they knew who they were. And while most English translations describe these two as "common" men, the idea of "common" or "ordinary" entirely misses the meaning of *idiotes*.

No, the leaders were amazed at them because, as Jesus' followers, they had become outsiders (*idiotes*), private people who no longer chose to participate in the religious life of the Jewish community.

The Logos

When I came to you, brothers, I did not come with excellence of **speech** or of wisdom as I told you about the secret purpose of God. **1 Corinthians 2:1**

❧❧❧

Speech: (LO'GOS λόγος) *n.*
a logical, specially-structured talk

The Speech

If an Athenian citizen became concerned about an issue that had arisen in the city, he could bring the matter before the assembly in the form of a speech. But he couldn't just talk about the problem—he also had to present a possible solution.

Since every citizen had the right to speak at assembly meetings, they had to set a time limit on the speeches so that a speaker wouldn't drone on and on. So, they used a water clock, called a *clepsydra*, for keeping time, and each speaker got just six minutes. This six-minute speech, which became known as the *logos*, had five required elements:

1. Reason—*the problem statement; what the issue is*
2. Wisdom—*a proposed solution with supporting arguments*
3. Expression—*a clear, logically-articulated presentation*
4. Persuasion—*why this is important; a call to action*
5. Credentials—*who I am; why you should listen to me*

When it was his turn to speak, the speaker walked up to a platform that was only one step higher than the ground. This small stage was called a *bema*, the Greek word for "step." Remember the *bema* in Philippi from which the Roman authorities spoke? This *bema* in Athens, from which ordinary people spoke, preceded it by 400 years and was the first *bema* in history,

Each speaker had to be well-prepared before he addressed the assembly. For if he was interrupted by the water clock before he was finished speaking, he would be asked to step down from the *bema* and would be publicly humiliated.

Over time, the function of this *logos* and *bema* transformed ordinary people—the butcher, the grocer, the man next door—into friends of wisdom and prepared the way for society to receive God's consummate *logos*, Jesus Christ, who is the reason, wisdom, expression, persuasion and credentials of God.

Two Voting Methods

And they cast **lots** for them, and the **lot** fell on Matthias, and he was counted with the eleven apostles. **Acts 1:26**

Lot: (KLER'OS κλήρος) *n.*
a randomly-selected black (no) or white (yes) stone

Also Practiced by the Church

Another thing that made Athenian citizens unique was the freedom they had to participate in city government. And while the assembly resolved the major issues facing Athens, city government handled its day-to-day affairs.

All adult males had the right to become candidates for the offices of government, whether in finance, administration, the courts or in other departments. In this small way, ordinary citizens could become "rulers" of their own city, so to speak. This freedom to hold public office deepened the responsibility Athenians felt for their city.

Government office holders were chosen once a year using a voting machine called a *kleroterion* (page 140). The candidates' names were written on metal slats that were inserted into slots in the machine. Black and white stones were randomly inserted into the top of the machine and if a *white stone* dropped out at the bottom, the candidate was approved. But if a *black stone* appeared, the candidate was disqualified. (In Rev 2:17, we find Jesus demonstrating his approval of his overcomers by giving them a *white stone*).

The early church used a similar random selection process when the Apostles replaced Judas Iscariot (Acts 1:26). In that instance, after they had prayed, the *kleros* fell to Matthias.

The only governmental positions that were not filled by random selection were the military and financial officers. Since these men were responsible for leading the army, executing foreign policy and managing the financial affairs of the city, these positions required specific skills and training. So, to elect generals, qualified candidates were first proposed to the citizens, who then voted for them publicly by lifting up their hands.

This kind of open voting, known in Greek as *cheirotoneo*, was also used in the New Testament for appointing elders in the churches (Acts 14:23), where it literally means, *choosing by the raising of hands*.

Ostracizing

Ought you not rather have mourned, so that the man who did this deed would be removed from your midst? For though I am absent in body, I am present in spirit; and I have already **passed judgment on** the one who did this, just as though I were present.

1 Corinthians 5:2–3

❧❧❧

Passed judgment on: (KRI'NO κρίνω) *v.*
judged, condemned

Protecting the Assembly

While the two types of voting we just spoke about were voluntary, there was a third kind of voting that was mandatory. All citizens were required to participate. This was a special voting process, designed to protect the democracy itself.

Once a year, at the time when the elections were held, the town erected an iron fenced-in area in the *agora* into which every citizen threw a broken piece of pottery with a name written on it—the name of the person who they thought threatened their democracy the most.

Now, who do you think would be considered "dangerous" to the Athenian society? The most popular person, of course! Someone who could speak convincingly in the assembly; someone who could persuade the citizens to adopt his proposals, but who might also lead them in the wrong direction.

After the voting ended, the individual whose name was written down most often (over a minimum of 6,000 votes) was taken into custody, exiled to the borders of the state and confined there for ten years until his popularity was neutralized. Then he could return.

Since the broken pieces of pottery that were used in this process are called *ostracon* in Greek, this type of voting became known as *ostracizing*, the act of removing a dangerous person from the group.

This third kind of voting appears in 1 Corinthians. When Paul, who was in Ephesus, learned that a particularly sinful brother was still in fellowship with the church, he urged the members to remove him from their midst (*ostracize* him). And since Paul couldn't be present to cast his vote, though his participation was mandatory, he joined them in spirit, having already voted for this action (1 Cor 5:2-3).

Sometime later, presumably after this brother's sinful influence had been neutralized by repentance, Paul considered the punishment "by the majority" to be sufficient and urged the believers to forgive him, comfort him and reaffirm their love for him (2 Cor 2:6-8).

The Ekklesia at Pnyx

And I say to you, you are Peter, and on this rock I will build my **church**. **Matthew 16:18**

❧❧❧

Church: (EKKLESI'A 'εκκλησια) *n.*
an assembly of the called-out ones

The Assembly of the Called-Out Ones

When we see many of the concepts of Athenian democracy showing up in the New Testament—the body, the *logos*, the *bema*, the *agora*, the three kinds of voting—we're amazed at the extent to which Greek culture informed the Scriptures and impacted the early church. Even the Greek word for church (*ekklesia*) is related to Athens.

The assembly of Athens met in the *agora* until 500 BC. But when the town square became too crowded and busy for meetings, the citizens looked for a different gathering place. They searched for a quiet location outside the residential area but safely within the city walls.

The place they chose was the top of a flat rock behind Mars Hill (page 125) called the Hill of Pnyx. Once they had leveled the site, they moved the meetings there.

When it was time for the assembly to meet, town criers went out into the city to call the people out of their residences. In Greek, the word *ek* means, "out" and *kaleo* is the verb, "to call." For this reason, the gatherings that were held on top of the rock became known as the *ekklesia,* "the meetings of the called-out ones."

What is the church? It too is an *ekklesia*, a gathering together of God's called-out ones—both locally and universally—those He has called out of this world.

Jesus was the first person in the New Testament to use the term *ekklesia* in this way (Matt 16:18). He made his "church announcement" in Caesarea Philippi, a Greek city in northern Israel founded by Alexander the Great and his successors. The city was originally named, Panias, since it was dedicated to Pan, the god of the shepherds.

There, in the place where the temple of the god of shepherds once stood, the Great Shepherd introduced his own flock, his own *ekklesia*, linking the word to the illustration of the rock.

And unlike the called-out assembly in Athens which was established on a natural rock, Jesus' *ekklesia* would be built on a spiritual rock, the revelation that he is the Christ, the Son of the living God.

Greek Philosophy

For as I went around and observed your objects of worship, I found also an altar on which was inscribed, 'To an **unknown** god.' So what you worship without knowing, this I proclaim to you. **Acts 17:23**

❧❧❧

Unknown: (AG'NOSTOS 'ἄγνωστος) *adj.*
without knowledge of, agnostic

The Unknown God

From our conversations about Athenian democracy, we now turn our attention to the development of Greek philosophy. Beginning in the 6th century BC, we have the rise of ancient Greek philosophy in Ionia (today's western Turkey). There we see the first *naturalistic* philosophers—men who searched for truth by thinking about *nature.*

These early thinkers looked at the natural world around them and were amazed by its complexity and beauty. As they studied the heavens and the earth, without the aid of telescopes and microscopes, they discovered that all of nature, from the smallest part to the largest, is one interconnected whole, pieces joined together like links in a chain.

And further, they found that nature is a unity, it obeys the laws of harmony and can be expressed mathematically. In fact, as they considered the dimensions of living things—plants, animals, people—they noticed that their shapes tended to follow the same mathematical formula (2x+1/x), which they called "the divine ratio."

This led them to conclude that nature, this unity, must itself be a created thing, an artifact. So, they called it *cosmos* (a jewel). Then, they asked, "Who created this artifact? Who is the artist, the jewel maker?" Their conclusion was that one or more "Great Minds" must have created nature, mathematical minds, parallel to our human minds.

Next, they asked, "Is there one Artist or more than one?" To answer this question, they considered how artwork is created. Since each artist sees reality differently, they said, different artists have different points of view. And since different points of view destroy harmony, these thinkers concluded that behind the *cosmos,* this harmonious jewel of nature, there must be only one—and not many—great mathematical mind.

So, knowing nothing else about this creator, they called him, "the Great Mathematical Mind." And since they could not identify him among the known mythological gods of the Greek religion, we have the beginning of the concept of "the unknown god."

Xenophanes and Parmenides

Jesus said to him, "I am the **way**, and the truth, and the life. No one comes to the Father except through me." **John 14:6**

❧❧❧

Way: (HODOS' ὁδός) *n.*
road, course, path

The Way, the Truth and the Life

At the end of the 6th century BC, a special man named Xenophanes lived in the city of Colophon in Ionia during very troubled times. When Xenophanes was 25 years old, the Persians attacked Asia Minor and he was forced to flee to southern Italy. There, together with other refugees, he built a new Greek city, Elea, and founded a philosophical school which would build on the ideas of the naturalistic thinkers.

Xenophanes would become famous for three "firsts." One, he was the first philosopher to criticize the Greek poets Homer and Hesiod for attributing human characteristics to the gods in their poems, including human sins and imperfections. To Xenophanes, this was outrageous. "How could any divine being be sinful or defective?" he said.

Two, Xenophanes was the first philosopher to speak about the unity of the divine nature. "If the divine being is everywhere and almighty," he argued, "there cannot be many gods, but one."

And three, as he considered the world around him, Xenophanes concluded that since all created things perish, everything that we can see, hear and feel is not actually "real." Only one thing is real, and that is the Creator of nature, the truly existing being. And for the first time in the history of philosophy, he called this real One, "the Being" (Ων).

One of Xenophanes' disciples, Parmenides, took these ideas and extended them further still. He said, "Since this Great Mathematical Mind is "the Being," he is, therefore, the spring of *truth* and the origin of *life*. So, for human beings, there *is* only one *way* for us to orient ourselves, and that *way* is towards him." In other words, "the Being" must be the *way*, the *truth* and the *life* for every human.

These philosophical thoughts became a part of Greek culture, the culture of the Mediterranean world at the time of Christ. So, when Jesus taught, he not only fulfilled the promises and prophecies of the Old Testament, he also confirmed the inquiries of these ancient Greek thinkers, here declaring to them, "I am the *way*, the *truth* and the *life*. No one comes to the Father except through me."

Socrates

I have called you **friends**, because all that I have heard from my Father I have made known to you. **John 15:15**

ᘓ ᘓ ᘓ

Friend: (PHI'LOS φίλος) *n.*
dear one, associate

The Good

According to Plato, when Parmenides was 65 years old, he traveled to Athens where he met a young man named Socrates, whom Greeks would one day consider to be the greatest of their philosophers.

At a time when Athens was the center of culture, knowledge and education of the Mediterranean world, we see a barefoot, poorly dressed man, wandering the streets of the city, telling everyone, "I know only one thing—that I know nothing!" This is Socrates.

Because Socrates believed that he "knew nothing," he never thought of himself as a teacher, nor of his followers as disciples. Instead, he called them "friends." And rather than passing along knowledge to his friends, he would ask them challenging questions and make them take positions on issues. This approach, which became known as the Socratic Method, turned the known teaching techniques of his time upside down.

In the Gospels, we see Jesus doing these same things, calling his disciples "friends" (John 15:15) and teaching them in this same way. Jesus would often open his conversations with questions or answer their questions with some of his own (see Matt 16:13-15).

Socrates became famous for making the search for "the good" the purpose of his life. It turns out that in Greek, there are two words for *good*. One is *kalos*, a word that describes how something appears on the outside—that which makes it seem attractive or beautiful.

Agathos, the second type of *good*, is different. *Agathos* is a virtuous inner quality which never feels the need to advertise itself or make itself known. It is *good* simply because it is *good*. Socrates sought *agathos*.

In the end, Socrates concluded that the *agathos* is not a subjective quality that can be found inside people. Rather, *agathos* is something objective that can only be found outside of us. And when people find "the *good*," they must then direct their lives towards it.

Jesus would one day confirm these ideas, saying, "No one is *agathos* except one—God... go, sell whatever you have... and come, follow me." (Mark 10:18,21).

Euclides of Megara

And as he was going out on the road, a man ran up, and kneeling before him, asked him, "**Good** teacher, what must I do to inherit eternal life?" But Jesus said to him, "Why do you call me **good**? No one is **good** except one—God." **Mark 10:17-18**

❧❧❧

Good: (AGATHOS' 'αγαθός) *adj.*
intrinsically virtuous

The Final Link in the Chain

At the beginning of Acts 18, when Paul leaves Athens to go to Corinth, he will pass by the city of Megara, a place that in antiquity was made famous by the Megarian philosophical school. This school was established by a disciple of Socrates, a man named Euclides of Megara.

Although Socrates spent his lifetime searching for the objective good, he was sentenced to death by the Athenian society for corrupting the youth and for introducing strange gods. As he promoted a lifestyle of seeking virtue among the young men of Athens, Socrates was accused of taking them away from their responsibilities to their families, homes and jobs to become lazy. For this reason, he was put to death.

Socrates' execution caused Plato and many of his other disciples to fear for their lives. So, they left Athens, went to Megara and found refuge in Euclides' home. After a while, when things settled down a bit, Euclides and others established a school of philosophy at Megara.

While at this school, Euclides linked Socrates' ideas of the *agathos*, "the objective good," with the philosophical approach to understanding divinity that was developed by Xenophanes, Parmenides and others.

By combining their concepts with his own, Euclides completed the chain of thought that joined the Great Mind, the unknown god, the Being, and the way, the truth and the life with the *agathos*, the Good. What is Good (*agathos*), Euclides concluded, must be God.

The chain was now complete.

Naturalistic philosophers—*the Great Mind*
Naturalistic philosophers—*the unknown God*
Xenophanes—*the Being*
Parmenides—*the way, the truth, the life*
Socrates—*the Good*
Euclides—*God*

Stoics and Epicureans

Also some of the Epicurean and Stoic philosophers were conversing with him, and some were asking, "What does this babbler want to say?" Others said, "He seems to be a proclaimer of strange gods," for he was announcing the good news about Jesus and the **resurrection**. **Acts 17:18**

❧❧❧

Resurrection: (ANASTA'SIS 'ανάστασις) *n.*
a raising up, a rising up

The Resurrection Rejecters

Having established the cultural and philosophical context of Athens, we are now ready to rejoin the story of Paul's missionary journey as he visits this special city (Acts 17:14-34).

Paul has just left Berea, having been persecuted there by fanatical Jews, and arrives in Athens. As he waits for his co-workers Silas and Timothy to join him, he converses with the Jews in the synagogue and people he meets in the *agora*, including the Stoics and the Epicureans, members of two opposing philosophical sects.

Though these groups had entirely different beliefs, they shared one thing in common—they both rejected the idea of resurrection.

The Stoics were descendants of Plato, Socrates and others who held that the soul is the essential part of the human being. Our bodies, then, are precious gifts, given to us by the gods, as temporary residences of our souls. But when we became sinners, our lives turned into lives of pain, struggles and death and our bodies turned into awful prisons.

Because of this, the Stoics believed that people should suffer life's punishments *stoically*—with patience and without complaint—until the gods have mercy on us and set us free from our prisons. When this happens, our death day, not our birthday, becomes our most joyful day, our day of freedom. So, for Paul to tell the Stoics about the resurrection of the body was like telling them to go back to prison.

The Epicureans, on the other hand, were materialists. To them, all this talk about gods, spirits and human souls was nonsense. Therefore, "let us eat, drink and be merry, for tomorrow we die" (1 Cor 15:32). Here we have the roots of a hedonistic lifestyle that only cares about today. So, to tell these people about resurrection would be foolishness.

Yet, when members of these two groups heard a foreigner speaking of a God who became a human, died and then resurrected bodily, they were intrigued by these strange new ideas. Eager to hear more from Paul, they brought him to the top of a nearby hill.

Mars Hill

And they took hold of him and brought him to the **Aeropagus** saying, "May we know what is this new teaching being presented by you? For you bring some strange things to our ears, so we want to know what these things mean." **Acts 17:19**

❧❧❧

Aeropagus: (AR'EIOS PAG'OS Ἄρειος Πάγος) *n.*
Ares' hill, Mars' hill

The Philosophers' Place

Mars Hill is a large outcropping of rock that sits 60 feet above the *agora*, just west of the Acropolis. Its name is the product of legend. According to a myth, Ares, the Greek god of war (*Mars* to Romans) was put on trial for the murder of Poseidon's son. This rock was the place the gods chose to hold this trial. It became known as Mars Hill.

In the 7th century BC, when the king-priest of Athens decided to abandon his administrative duties, he delegated them to a committee of nobles. In time, this body also took on judicial responsibilities. This group left the Acropolis and came down to a lower place to hold their meetings. Mars Hill was that place. So, they called themselves the Mars Hill Committee.

Two centuries later, during the time of the Athenian democracy, most of the governmental authority of this committee transferred to the people, except the judicial authority. At that time, they served as the Supreme Court of Athens, hearing only the most serious cases, mostly murder cases. Court was held on Mars Hill. The rock was surrounded by a retaining wall, and a platform was built on a leveled section. The judges would sit on this platform with the accusers on one side of them, the accused on the other and the public watching.

The reason why court was held out in the open, under the sky, was to give the gods the opportunity to intervene on the side of the accused should he be innocent and wrongly charged.

Because capital cases were so rare in those days, the city opened Mars Hill to the public. During the day, townspeople could come up from the *agora* to get away from the busyness, and in the evenings, to sit and watch the sunset.

And since Mars Hill was a quiet place, it became a popular place for philosophers to meet and debate ideas. People who were interested in following these debates could come and watch.

In Acts 17:19-20, the philosophers brought Paul to Mars Hill, ascending the hand-chiseled stone steps to the top, to hear what this babbler had to say.

The Stoa of Attalos

By the hands of the apostles many signs and wonders were being done among the people. And they were all together in Solomon's **Portico.** **Acts 5:12**

❧❧❧

Portico: (STO'A στοά) *n.*
a building with at least one long, open colonnade

The Model for Solomon's Porch

On his way up to Mars Hill, Paul would have passed by a building on the eastern edge of the *agora* called the Stoa of Attalos.

Attalos, the king of Pergamum, erected this beautiful structure in the 2nd century BC to express his gratitude to the city of Athens for the education he and his family had received there. The building was made of limestone with marble facades and columns. It became the primary shopping center of the *agora* and was used in this way for centuries.

Stoas, buildings designed with a wide colonnade (covered walkway or portico), first appeared in the 6th century BC. They were public gathering places that protected people from the rain and the strong Mediterranean sun, while giving them the impression that they were still outside. This was important for the public life of the Greeks, a people who had a love affair with nature. The Stoics, who years later met in a *stoa*, took their name from this type of building.

According to the Hebrew historian Josephus, Herod the Great, the king who rebuilt the temple in Jerusalem, was a fanatic Hellenist. So, he adopted a Greek architectural style when he lavishly restored the temple. As one example, the marble road that surrounded Herod's temple copied the *peripatos* (walkway) that encircled the Acropolis in Athens.

Herod enclosed the temple's main entrance with a *stoa* that was modeled after the Stoa of Attalos. This section of his temple became known as Solomon's Porch. It was the area where the temple's buying and selling took place (Matt 21:12).

Solomon's Porch was also the place where Jesus taught much of the time (John 10:23) and where the Sanhedrin (Jewish council) held their meetings. The first church, the church in Jerusalem, also used this *stoa* for its gatherings (Acts 5:12).

Today, the *stoa* of the temple in Jerusalem is totally destroyed. But if you were to stand in the Stoa of Attalos, reconstructed in 1952, with its lofty roof and open columns, you would feel what it must have been like to meet where the first church met.

Paul's Mars Hill Speech

So Paul, **standing** in the midst of the Aeropagus said: "Men of Athens, I perceive that in every way you are a very devout people." **Acts 17:22**

❧❧❧

Standing: (HIS'TEMI 'ἵστημι) *v.*
taking a stand

His Two-Minute Logos

The Stoic and Epicurean philosophers who spoke with Paul in the *agora* wanted to hear more from him. So, they brought him to their meeting place on the top of Mars Hill, and said, "May we know what is this new teaching being presented by you? For you bring some strange things to our ears, so we want to know what these things mean" (Acts 22:19-20).

Much like the men of Athens who prepared their six-minute *logos* to address the assembly, Paul structured his speech to these intellectual, philosophical Greeks logically.

Since his hearers didn't much care for the Hebrew Scriptures, Paul didn't build his talk on Old Testament facts like Stephen did in his defense before a Jewish audience (Acts 7:1-42). No, he addressed them philosophically, by speaking to their concept of "the unknown god" (Acts 17:22-31).

This God, said Paul, quoting two Greek poets, is the One who created the *cosmos*, the One who is not far from each one of us:

"In him we live and move about and exist." Cleanthes
"For we too are his offspring." Aratus

These two poets were not well known. Why not quote the brilliant Athenian minds like Socrates, Plato or Sophocles? Possibly, like a seasoned Athenian orator, Paul was building his six-minute *logos* from the least to the greatest, following the highest speech-making standards of his day.

If you read Paul's ten-verse speech out loud, timing yourself with a stopwatch, you'll see that it took Paul about two minutes to get to this point. In that short time, Paul had led his audience all the way from the creation of the world to Jesus, God's appointed Judge. But as soon as Paul mentioned Christ's resurrection from the dead, these resurrection rejecters stopped him and dismissed the meeting.

No doubt, in the remaining four minutes of his *logos*, Paul could have continued God's redemptive story from the resurrection to the end of the age, a complete presentation of God's eternal plan.

Paul Makes Tents

After this Paul **departed** from Athens and went to Corinth.
Acts 18:1

ঌ ঌ ঌ

Departed from: (CHORI'ZO χωρίζω) *v.*
separated himself from

His Abrupt Departure

At the end of Acts 17, following his interrupted speech, a number of men and women believed and joined themselves to Paul, including Dionysus the Areopagite (a member of the Supreme Council) and a woman by the name of Damaris.

Then, rather abruptly, Paul *departed from* Athens and went to Corinth. Though his preaching had been successful, and though Athens was the only place in Greece where he was not persecuted, Paul seems to have left the city in a quite a hurry (Acts 18:1).

Why was he so eager to get to Corinth, a city of prostitutes, the place where he would soon experience fear (1 Cor 2:3)? The answer is that he wanted to arrive in time for the Isthmian Games, the inter-Greek athletic events that were being held in Corinth that year.

These games brought Greeks from across the Mediterranean world to Corinth. Only the Olympic games were more important. Paul rushed out of Athens because of these games.

How do we know this? First, Paul was a tentmaker (Acts 18:3). And history tells us that during the games, most competitors and spectators preferred to stay close to the athletic venues, which were located about three miles from the city, and live there in tents.

Acts says that the first thing Paul did when he got to Corinth was to join two tentmakers, Aquila and Priscilla and start making tents. Paul had hurried to Corinth to make tents for these visitors.

Second, the Gallio inscription in Delphi confirms that Gallio was in Corinth in the Spring of AD 51 and we know from the Bible that Paul arrived in Corinth shortly *before* Gallio was named proconsul. History also confirms that the Isthmian Games were held during the summer of that same year.

So, Paul hurried out of Athens, not because he was kicked out of the city, nor because he had failed. No. This missionary preacher went to Corinth to share the gospel with the thousands of people coming into the city from all over the world, from places Paul might never visit.

Eleusis

Now to him who is able to establish you according to my gospel and the preaching of Jesus Christ, according to the **revelation** of the **mystery** that has been kept **secret** for long ages past, but is now manifested. **Romans 16:25–26**

On our way from Athens to the spectacular archaeological site at Corinth, our tour makes a brief stop at the ancient town of Eleusis, world famous for its mysterious religious rites. Here we will discover how, from these pagan ceremonies, Jesus, Paul and others brought important ideas and rich language into the New Testament.

The Mysteries

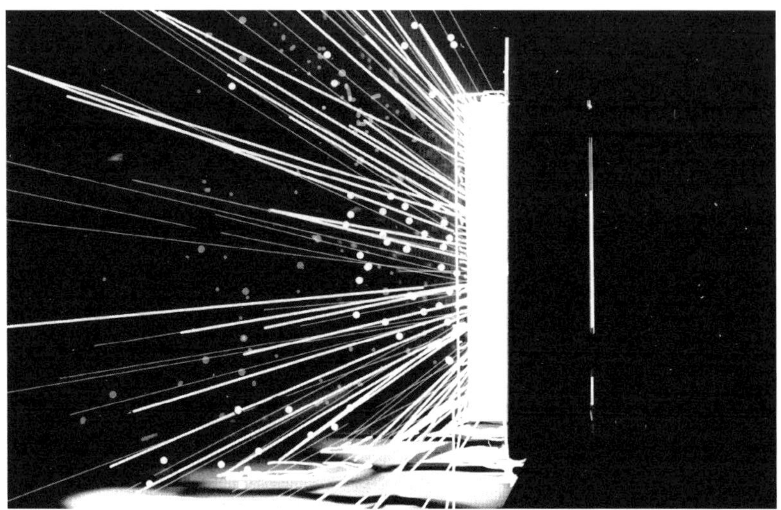

And he said to them, "To you has been given the **mystery** of the kingdom of God, but to those outside, everything is in parables."
Mark 4:11–12

❧❧❧

Mystery: (MYSTE'RION μυστήριον) *n.*
secret, sacred truth transmitted in a personal, experiential way

The Picture of the Kingdom of God

When Paul traveled from Athens to Corinth, he walked west along a road that had been in use for centuries. The first 20 kilometers of this road connected Athens with the town of Eleusis, where secret ceremonies known as "the mysteries" took place.

These unusual religious rites, which were held once a year for more than 1,500 years, initiated people into the society of Demeter and Persephone, a group that claimed to possess special knowledge of the afterlife. Through mysterious ceremonies, this knowledge was revealed to the celebrants, answering for them the existential question, "What happens to people when they leave this world?"

Initiation into the mysteries was open to all people—Greek or foreigner, man or woman, free or slave—as long as they understood the Greek language and swore to abide by a strict code of silence. Participants included some Roman Emperors, who even though they were worshiped as gods, wanted to know what would happen to them after they died.

Those who chose to participate in these rites were different than "those who were outside," as the uninitiated were called. Most were moral people who hoped that the initiation would change their lives in this world for the better. Since they believed in an afterlife, they also trusted that the effects of these rites would help them earn a place of happiness in the world to come.

We know that Jesus knew about "the mysteries" and what they meant to participants by the words he spoke during his ministry. In fact, Jesus introduced the term *mystery* into the New Testament when he began to speak in parables, knowing that this word would transport his hearers' minds back to these ancient Greek ceremonies.

In like fashion, by teaching in parables, Jesus could reveal the secrets of the kingdom of God to his disciples, those who were initiated into his heavenly kingdom, while keeping the secret things of God hidden from the indifferent masses who were "outside."

Secret Ceremonies

To those outside, everything is in **parables**, so that when they look, they may **see** and not perceive, and when they listen, they may **hear** and not understand; otherwise they might **turn** and be forgiven. **Mark 4:11–12**

❧❧❧

Parable: (PARABOLE' παραβολή) *n.*
something laid alongside

See, Hear and Do

The initiation into the mysteries followed three stages. The first was a teaching phase which took place in Athens during the springtime. People who were to be inducted in the Fall came to Athens in the Spring to be taught by the priests from Eleusis in a temple built in the 5th century BC not far from the Acropolis.

Then, these celebrants returned to Athens in September to take part in phase two which consisted of purification ceremonies with fastings, washing in the sea and offering sacrifices. During this time, the high priestess of Demeter and a group of Eleusinian priests prepared a special box into which they placed the mysteries' sacred, secret elements.

When all was ready, the priests and initiates, escorted by officials of both cities, formed a procession and walked "The Sacred Way," the 20-kilometer distance from Athens to Eleusis, arriving in the afternoon. Then, they entered the temple of Demeter and the sacred ceremonies began, rites which lasted the entire night until daybreak.

Because of the strict secrecy of their society, we don't know many of the details of what happened that night. But we do know that for the initiates the experience was extremely shocking and intense. We also know that the rituals included three activities.

First, the people *heard* sacred words spoken. Then, the sacred box was opened, and the celebrants *saw* the holy elements inside. Finally, they participated in some kind of drama, *acting* out a story, possibly the story of Hades, Persephone and Demeter. So, during this ceremony, the people *heard, saw* and *acted.*

In Mark 4:10-12, when Jesus explained his first parable to his disciples, he quoted Isaiah 6:9-10. There, the prophet said that someday people would *see* but not perceive, would *hear* but not understand, and would not *act* to repent. It may not be coincidence that these three mysterious outcomes map directly to the segments of the Eleusinian initiation.

The Kiste

That by **revelation** the mystery was made known to me.
Ephesians 3:3

❧❧❧

Revelation: (APOKAL'YPSIS 'αποκάλυψις) *n.*
taking the cover off, an unveiling

Seeing Inside the Box

The special box that held the mysteries' sacred, secret items was a circular container called a *kiste*, which looked like a decorated cake. The high priestess of Demeter led the procession of celebrants from Athens to Eleusis balancing the *kiste* on top of her head.

Later that night, at the height of the initiation, the priests helped her uncover the box, revealing its secret contents for all the celebrants to see. This "seeing inside the box" would later be described by the Greek verb *apokalypto*. Since *kalypto* means "to cover," *apokalypto* means "to uncover." This is the literal meaning of the English words, *reveal* and *revelation*. A revelation is an *apokalypsis*, from which we get the book title, *Apocalypse*, or Revelation.

Paul used the word *mystery* over 20 times in his writings, a term that was common among the Greeks, but was never used in the Old Testament. Just like Jesus, each time Paul gave the word a spiritual meaning when he wrote about:

the *mystery* of God (Col 2:2),
the *mystery* of Christ (Eph 3:4; Col 4:3),
the *mystery* of Christ and the church (Eph 5:32),
the *mystery* of godliness (1 Tim 3:16),

and other mysterious aspects of the kingdom of heaven. These deep things of God, known to Him alone, are revealed to his believers by his Spirit (1 Cor 2:10) for the purpose of furthering his kingdom.

Paul's most famous *mystery* reference is found in 1 Corinthians. Here he answers the question that was asked by the ancient Greeks, "What happens to people when they leave this world?"

> *Listen, I tell you a* **mystery**: *we will not all die, but we all will be changed—in an instant, in the twinkling of an eye, at the last trumpet. For the trumpet will sound, and the dead will be raised imperishable, and we will be changed.* **1 Cor 15:51**

The Stalk of Wheat

And Jesus answered (the Greeks), saying, "The hour has come for the Son of Man to be glorified. I tell you the solemn truth, unless a kernel of **wheat** falls into the ground and dies, it remains a single kernel; but if it dies it produces a great harvest."

John 12:23–24

❧❧❧

Wheat: (SI'TOS σῖτος) *n.*
primary bread-making grain of the Mediterranean people

Jesus Speaks to the Greeks

The Eleusinian mysteries, the most famous religious event in the Mediterranean region, finds its origin in Greek mythology in the story of the goddess Demeter and her daughter, Persephone.

According to this myth, one day, while Persephone was picking flowers with her friends, the earth suddenly cracked open beneath her and out flew Hades, the god of the underworld. Hades grabbed Persephone, pulling her into his chariot, abducting her, kicking and screaming, to the underworld, where he forced her to marry him.

As Demeter searched for her missing daughter, the Eleusinian people comforted her. In exchange for their kindness, Demeter gave them two precious gifts. One was the mysteries, and the other was a stalk of wheat, the mysteries' highest and most sacred symbol.

To experience the mysteries was like dying and being brought back to life again. The first part of the ritual took place in total darkness and was extremely frightening. The people believed that they had descended into the underworld and there had met Hades and Persephone.

But in the second part, as a light began to penetrate the darkness, the people began to feel hopeful and comforted. At this point, the priest gave each person a stalk of wheat as a symbol of their experience. From this, wheat soon became, for all Greeks, both the symbol of the mysteries and the sign of death and resurrection.

In John 12:20-24, in the last event of Jesus' public ministry, some devout Greeks wanted to see Jesus. So, they approached Philip to ask him to try to arrange this. Philip found Andrew (the only other disciple with a Greek name) and together they approached Jesus.

When Jesus saw the Greeks, he spoke to them about his death and resurrection by using a grain of wheat as his illustration. He was communicating with them in their own cultural language, knowing that by doing so, they would understand the meaning of his death and the new eternal life he would bring mankind in resurrection.

Corinth

After this Paul departed from Athens and went to **Corinth**.
Acts 18:1

The city of Corinth is the final destination of our journey following Paul's footsteps through Greece—and it's Paul 's final stop too. From here he sails home to Antioch. Through our visit to the archaeological site and museum in Corinth we'll gain an appreciation for the important role this infamous city played in Paul's ministry and see aspects of the city's history and life that appear in Paul's letters and the book of Acts.

Corinth and Acrocorinth

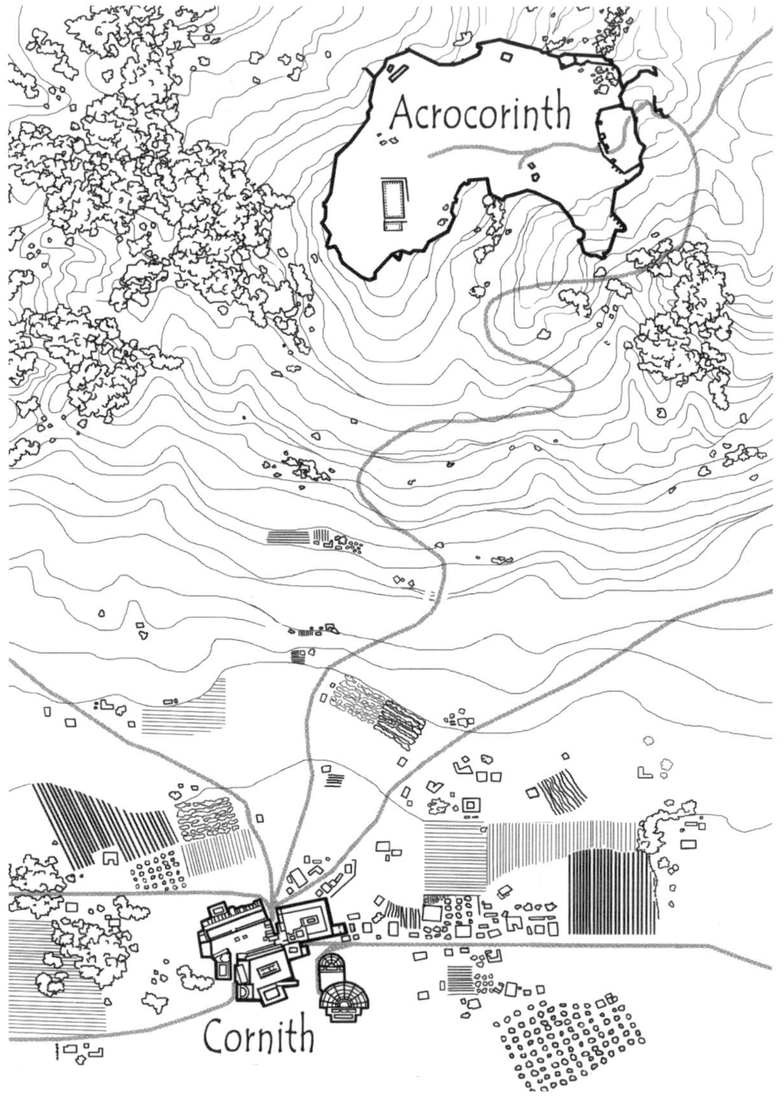

Ancient Corinth

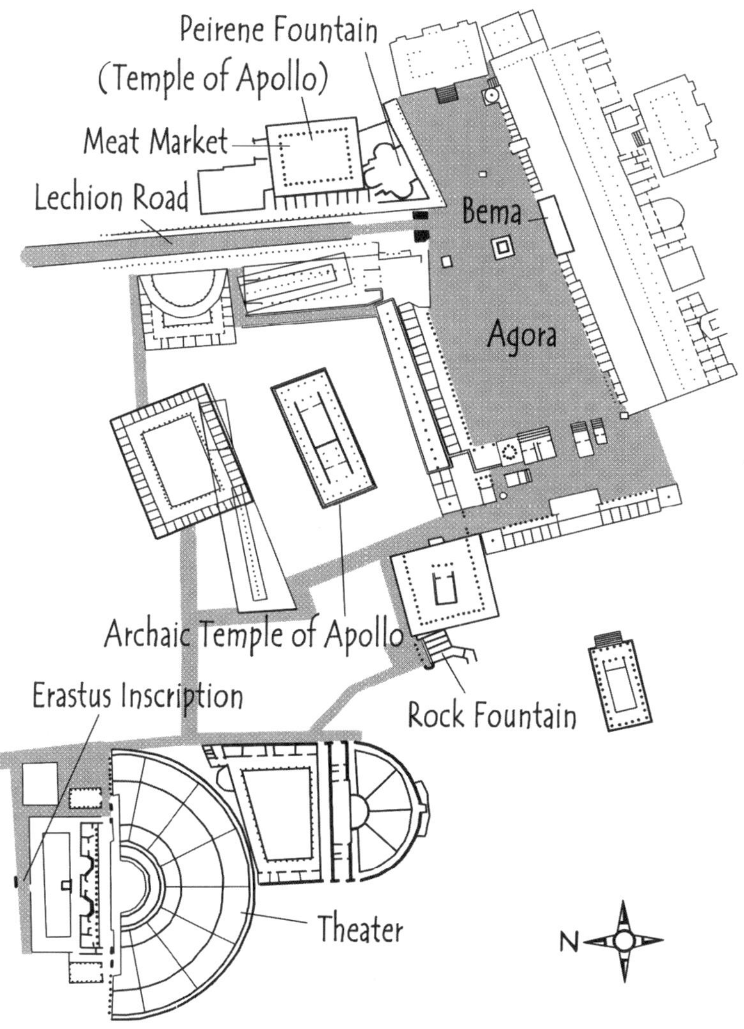

The Corinthianizing City

Do you not know that your bodies are members of Christ? Shall I then take the members of Christ and make them members of a **prostitute**. Never! **1 Corinthians 6:15**

❧❧❧

Prostitute: (POR'NE πόρνη) *n.*
harlot, unchaste female

Sin City on Steroids

Alexander's campaigns radically changed the Mediterranean world. Wherever his armies went, they built Greek cities, hundreds of them, the largest being Alexandria in Egypt.

Three of these cities, Alexandria, Antioch and Ephesus, were located at the end of major trade routes, all of which passed through Corinth on their way to Rome. This made Corinth the center of commercial transport, which, in turn, made the city very wealthy.

Twenty-five years after the Romans had conquered the Macedonians, the Roman Senate decided to punish those who resisted its power. In 146 BC, to teach the Empire a lesson, they ordered that two cities, Corinth and Carthage, should be leveled—should disappear.

When the Roman army arrived in Corinth, they destroyed most of the city. Some historians suggest that the Romans left certain Greek temples and public buildings standing. And as the solders plundered the city, they remarked that they had never seen such treasures.

When Julius Caesar came to power, he decided to rebuild Corinth. But before he could do so, he was assassinated. Under his successor, Octavian Augustus, the city regained its prominence. Its huge *agora*, the largest in the empire, was bigger than the Forum in Rome, and at Paul's time, was completely paved with marble.

The acropolis of the town, a massive mountain called Acrocorinth, rose 1,886 feet above the city itself. The temple of Aphrodite, the Greek goddess of love, occupied the top of this mountain and housed over 1,000 female temple slaves. These women practiced sacred prostitution as a form of worship to their goddess.

The temple slaves became *the* main attraction of the city. There was neither a rich ship owner nor a poor galley slave whose visit to Corinth did not include this kind of veneration of the goddess.

As a result, the city gained a notorious reputation for sexual license and a new word was coined. To "Corinthianize" meant to practice sex with abandon.

The Practice of Head Covering

Any (woman) who prays or prophesies with her head uncovered disgraces her head, for it is one and the same as a woman who has her head shaved. For if a woman will not **cover** her head, she should cut her hair short. But if it is disgraceful for a woman to have her hair cut short or have her head shaved, she should **cover** her head. **1 Corinthians 11:5–6**

❧❧❧

Cover: (KATAKALYP'TO κατακαλύπτω) *v.*
to entirely veil, to completely cover

An Expression of Paul's Great Love

Every day, as you looked up from Corinth to Acrocorinth, you could see a procession of female slaves from Aphrodite's temple zig-zagging their way down the mountainside to offer the Corinthians and visitors the opportunity to "worship" the goddess through them.

As a way of attracting attention to themselves, these women carved the words "Follow Me" on the bottoms of their sandals. Then, as they walked along the dusty streets, this phrase was imprinted on the ground. Anyone who wanted to find them could easily follow their footprints.

To help people recognize them from a distance, these ladies did something even more dramatic. They shaved their heads. This was as shocking to the Corinthians then as it would be to us today.

Throughout history, while it was not unusual for a man to have short hair, for women, it was entirely a different thing. Since a woman's hair displayed her honor and beauty, having short hair was dishonoring. After WWII, for example, French women who were found working for the Nazi's had their heads shaved. And still today, in some countries, a woman who is caught committing adultery has her hair cut off.

Paul visited Corinth at least three times. During his first visit, he stayed there a year and a half. There is little doubt that Paul had seen these bald-headed ladies many times. Surely, some of them heard him preach the message of salvation and accepted it.

So, in order to create a safe place for these new believers, Paul asked all women at church meetings to *completely cover* their heads with scarves (*katakalypto*). This gave all women in the church an equal standing and became the cultural reason behind the practice of head covering.

While it may have been easy for Paul to get temple workers to cover their bald heads, it was probably quite difficult for him to persuade the "proper" women to cover theirs. So, to convince them, Paul uplifted the practice by giving it a spiritual and symbolic meaning (1 Cor 11:7-12). But for him, head covering was never a matter of doctrine. Rather, it was the expression of his great love for these new converts.

The Erastus Inscription

Erastus the city **treasurer** greets you… **Romans 16:23**

ᘓ ᘓ ᘓ

Treasurer: (OIKONOM'OS οἰκονόμος) *n.*
a fiscal agent, a steward

The Treasurer of Corinth

Paul wrote his letter to the Romans from Corinth. In the closing verses of this letter, he sends greetings to the Roman Christians from a man by the name of Erastus, the Treasurer of Corinth (Rom 16:23).

During the 1800's, this verse became controversial when a group of German scholars known as the "higher critics" said that it couldn't be true. These same "scholars" suggested that the Bible is a collection of legends written by ordinary men and shouldn't be taken literally.

They believed that Paul's followers were a Jewish sect made up of the poor and slaves. Because of this, they argued, it would have been impossible for Paul to have known the Treasurer of Corinth at all, much less that this person would have become a Christian.

Further, they claimed that since Erastus is a very rare Greek name which doesn't appear on any historical records of Corinthian treasurers, he never existed. Rather, Paul had fabricated this person to impress his uneducated Roman readers in advance of his planned trip to Rome.

In Paul's day, since a city treasurer had the responsibility for managing the public wealth, he held a high office. Cities often selected the well-to-do for this role, believing that rich people would both know how to manage money and be less likely to steal public funds.

Since most treasurers were honorable men, at the end of their terms of service, they often expressed their gratitude to their cities by giving back a lasting monument of some kind—a fountain, a building, a road, a statue—as a token of their appreciation.

In 1929, as archaeologists were excavating the site of the theater in Corinth, they unearthed the pavement of the ancient city's road. On the sidewalk next to this road they discovered an inscription from the person who had donated the road to the city. The English translation of this Latin inscription reads:

> *I, Erastus, the Treasurer of the city, laid this pavement at my own expense as a sign of my gratitude to the city.*

Paul and the truth of the New Testament were vindicated!

The Temple of Aphrodite

Or do you not know that your body is a temple of the Holy Spirit who is in you, whom you have received from God, and you are not your own? For you were **bought** with a price; therefore glorify God with your body. **1 Corinthians 6:19–20**

❧❧❧

Bought: (AGORA'ZO 'αγοράζω) *v.*
purchased, acquired, redeemed

Mr. Sexy Redeems the Temple Slaves?

The money that the temple slaves brought in from the worshippers of Aphrodite went to support the operations of the temple and made the sanctuary very rich. And since these ladies were slaves, they were the property of the temple.

When some of these women became Christians, they would have faced a problem. Though they may have a new-found desire to leave the temple service to become members of the church, this couldn't happen unless someone "redeemed" them.

That someone must walk up to the temple and have a financial conversation with the high priestess. The person might say, "Dear lady, tell me how much money you want for this person and for that person and for that person..."

And because we are speaking about redeeming slaves, that someone would not have negotiated with the high priestess over price, which would have been quite high.

It would have taken a very rich man to do this. Without a doubt, the church in Corinth had at least one person who would have fit the bill, financially speaking—the Treasurer, Erastus, who was, most likely, the richest citizen of the city. And though we don't have biblical or historical evidence to prove that Erastus purchased freedom for these temple slaves, I believe that he did.

Paul uses similar temple-and-slave language in 1 Cor 6:19-20 to speak theologically of Christ's purchase of sinners with the price he paid by his death on the cross. But for the temple slaves in Corinth whose freedom was purchased by a Christian redeemer, the words, "you were bought with a price" would have carried a very practical meaning.

Ironically, the name Erastus literally means, "one worthy to be loved *erotically*." This name is a derivative of the Greek word *eros* and can be translated into the English word, *sexy*. We could see the divine humor in the supposition that a Greek man named "Sexy" would be used by God to deliver sex slaves into His church.

The Hetaera

If (women) want to find out about something, they should ask their own husbands at home; for it is improper for a woman to **speak** in church. **1 Corinthians 14:35**

❧❧❧

Speak: (LALE'O λαλέω) *v.*
to use the mouth a lot

Women Speaking in Church

Paul wrote to the Corinthians that "it is *improper* for a woman to speak in church." But why did he say this?

In antiquity, women were always subservient to men. Back then, a proper married woman belonged to her husband. Her primary role was to take care of the household. If she ventured out of the house to go to the *agora*, she never went alone, but was always escorted by a male family member, even a boy or a slave.

Rarely did a married woman speak anywhere in public, and never to other men, unless she was spoken to. And when she responded, she would never make eye contact and only gave brief answers. If she wanted to discuss something more fully, she asked her husband at home.

In those days, education was always private, was mostly for boys and took place in the home. Sometimes, rich families who had slaves to do the domestic chores, offered their girls the opportunity to study music or listen when the teacher taught the boys.

In time, as these educated, affluent girls became women, many decided to pursue independent lifestyles out from under the authority of men. Some purchased homes, hired younger ladies to work for them and began offering Geisha-like services to affluent men, including discussions of various kinds, entertainment and high-class prostitution.

Soon, these emancipated females, who were called "the Hetaera" (colleagues), became men's companions and began to enjoy equivalent male privileges. They walked to the *agora* alone, where they behaved like men, spoke with them face to face and expressed their opinions publicly.

Though these ladies had the right to speak and had a lot to say, they were prostitutes. This is the first reason why Paul said, "it is *improper* for a woman to speak in church." Doing so would remind everyone of the Hetaera, especially in Corinth, the city of prostitutes.

The second reason is related to the first. The Greek word that Paul chose for *speak* doesn't simply mean, "to say something." It literally means "to talk at great length; to prattle; to use the mouth a lot."

The Bema of Corinth

But when Gallio was proconsul of Achaia, the Jews rose up with one accord against Paul and brought him before the **tribunal**, saying, "This man is persuading men to worship God in a way contrary to the law." Gallio said... "See to it yourselves. I do not wish to be a judge of these matters." And he drove them from the **tribunal**. **Acts 18:12–16**

❧❧❧

Tribunal: (BE'MA βῆμα) *n.*
a raised platform, a grandstand

Gallio's Grandstand

The archaeological site at Corinth has been excavated down to the Roman period, the time of Apostle Paul. This means that the ground that visitors stand on is the very ground on which Paul once stood.

The *agora* in Corinth was the largest city square in the Empire. Small shops lined the commercial section of the square, while a large raised platform, the magnificent *bema* of Corinth, dominated the other side of the courtyard (see page 177). This limestone grandstand was overlaid with marble and was beautifully decorated.

The Roman proconsul Gallio, whose inscription we spoke about in Delphi, stood on this *bema* to participate in city events, reward local benefactors who were sympathetic to Rome, or publicly shame enemies.

As in Philippi, a pillar was placed in front of the *bema* with a metal ring on one side of it. A person who was charged with speaking against Rome or other treasonous activities was chained to this ring, his accusers standing around him, as allegations were made. If he was found guilty, he knelt down, his garments were removed, and as he embraced this pillar, he was flogged in the open in this most public part of the city.

In Acts 18, this was the place where Sosthenes, the moderating elder of the synagogue in Corinth, and a group of angry Jews brought Paul to stand before Gallio's tribunal (*bema*). As the Jews soon found out, this turned out to be a big mistake. Since the Jewish community was under the jurisdiction of the local authorities (not the provincial government), if local issues arose, the Jews were to take their problems there.

It seems that Sosthenes may have intentionally ignored the city authorities when he and the Jews brought Paul directly to Gallio. But since the governor's time was very precious, not just anyone could see him. And as Sosthenes began to raise questions about Jewish religious law, Gallio interrupted him and drove them all away from his *bema*.

Then, the Jews, having been publicly humiliated in front of the provincial governor, beat Sosthenes on the spot, in front of the *bema*, for his breach of proper protocol (Acts 18:17).

The Stone Pavement in Jerusalem

On hearing these words, Pilate brought Jesus out and sat down on the judge's bench (*bema*, Greek) in the place called "**Stone Pavement**," or in Hebrew, "Gabbatha." **John 19:13**

❧❧❧

Stone Pavement: (LITHOSTRO'TOS λιθόστρωτοσ) *n.*
a large area paved with stone blocks

An Agora, a Bema and a Pillar

During Roman times, *agoras* with their *bemas* and pillars could be found in cities across the Empire. But you may be surprised to learn that the city of Jerusalem also had an *agora*, *bema* and pillar.

In the 2nd century BC, after Israel came under Gentile control, Antiochus Epiphanes, a Hellenistic king, established a large *agora* in Jerusalem. He also erected temples to Zeus, Asclepius and other pagan gods and built a Greek gymnasium and a theater.

Because the *agora* in Jerusalem was not culturally relevant to the life of the Jews, they seldom referred to it as "the *agora*." For them, this wide area paved with limestone blocks was called "the Stone Pavement," or in the Hebrew, "Gabbatha," literally, "the place of the platform."

This is where Jesus' public trial took place (John 19:13; Matt 27:19) and is the first time that the word *bema* appears in the New Testament.

During the night when Jesus was betrayed, the Jewish leaders questioned Jesus thoroughly. Then, they brought him to Pilate, the Roman governor of Judea, at the Praetorium, his headquarters located beside the Stone Pavement. When Jesus entered the yard of the Praetorium, the Jews stayed outside, not wanting to defile themselves at Passover.

Inside the Praetorium yard, Pilate spoke with Jesus more than once before concluding that he had done nothing worthy of death. But to appease the Jews, before releasing him, Pilate had him scourged publicly. Most likely, the Roman soldiers chained Jesus to the pillar on the Stone Pavement in front the *bema* as in other Roman cities.

The Jews had originally claimed that Jesus should be put to death because he made himself equal with God. But when Pilate found no fault in him, the Jews changed their strategy. They dropped their religious charge and picked up a political one, claiming that Jesus had defied Caesar by making himself King.

When Pilate heard this, he came out of the Praetorium, sat on the *bema* and pronounced his judgment (John 19:13).

Acrocorinth

For the weapons of our warfare are not of the flesh, but are empowered by God for tearing down **strongholds.** We tear down arguments and every lofty idea that is raised against the knowledge of God. **2 Corinthians 10:4-5**

ঌ ঌ ঌ

Stronghold: (OCHU'ROMA 'οχύρωμα) *v.*
a castle, a rock-fortress

A Spiritual Stronghold

Next to the *agora*, on the corner where Corinth's main street meets the city center, stands the ruins of an ancient water source know as the Peirene Fountain. While the arches of this fountain are from the Roman period, the pillars date back to Classical times.

This spring-fed fountain continuously provided fresh water to area residents from very ancient times until World War II. For thousands of years, local people came here to fill up their water pots with cold, clean drinking water.

In front of the fountain was a shallow swimming pool which was used by the Corinthians to refresh themselves during hot summer days. Slaves from the temple of Aphrodite would often visit this place to collect "thirsty" worshippers.

As we mentioned earlier, this "high city" of Corinth stood on the top of a massive mountain not far from the city itself (see pages 176 and 178). The summit of this mountain was so large that an entire town could be built there. Because of the precipitous, insurmountable cliffs that protected Acrocorinth, the site had tremendous strategic military value. Years after Paul's stay in Corinth, the Roman Emperor Theodosius turned the mountaintop into a fortress.

But at the time of the Apostle Paul, this stronghold was not used by the military. Rather, because of the influence of the temple of Aphrodite, it was a *spiritual* stronghold used by the forces of evil. The sinful life of Corinth was interwoven with the activities of this place. Everything was under its dark shadow. In a very real sense, the spiritual forces of Acrocorinth controlled the city.

For this reason, when Paul wrote to the Corinthians about tearing down *strongholds* (2 Cor 10:4-5) he may have been thinking of this high city. Our spiritual weapons, says Paul, are not those of human warfare but are empowered by God to demolish spiritual strongholds, deceptive thoughts that rise up like impenetrable mountains.

The Meat Market

Eat whatever is sold in the **(meat market)**, asking no question based on conscience… However, if someone should say to you, "This has been offered in sacrifice," then do not eat it, for the sake of the one who told you. **1 Corinthians 10:25,28**

❧❧❧

Meat market: (MAKEL'LON μάκελλον) *n.*
a place to buy meat

Eating Meat Sacrificed to Idols

Not far from the Pierene Fountain, visitors to Corinth's archaeological site can see the ruins of Apollo's temple. The pillars from this sanctuary date back to the 6th century BC.

Like all ancient temples, including the Jewish temple in Jerusalem, the temple of Apollo was oriented west to east, its entrance facing the rising of the sun. In front of the temple was an altar. A rectangular pit outlines the place where the altar once stood.

The animals that were regularly offered as sacrifices to Apollo were brought here, slaughtered and divided into three portions. The inedible parts were given to the god and were burnt to ashes on the altar. The edible parts went to the offerors and the priests. After the sacrifice ended, the offerors partook of a sacred meal, where they received the title, "participants of the altar," a term that Paul used in 1 Cor 10:18.

Now, imagine what happened on Apollo's birthday when the entire city brought animals for sacrifice. Because of the volume, by the end of the day, the priests had collected huge quantities of high-quality meats that they had to get rid of quickly due to the lack of refrigeration.

The solution to this problem was to take this meat to the meat market (*makellon*) where it could be sold inexpensively. In those days, since animals were the capital that families owned, people rarely ate meat. Their diet was mostly vegetarian. So, this market provided people with a unique opportunity to enjoy low cost meat.

During the 1st century, though Christians were prohibited from participating in pagan festivals, a question arose in the church as to whether a believer should eat sacrificial meat that was purchased from this market. Paul directly addressed these concerns in his first letter to the Corinthians, writing that it's fine to eat this meat, but let your conscience and the circumstances guide you (1 Cor 10:25-36).

Paul's biblical mention of a meat market in Corinth was confirmed by a Latin inscription that was found during an excavation in 1898. This inscription now resides at the Corinth Museum.

The Rock Fountain

And all drank the same **spiritual** drink; for they used to drink from the **spiritual** rock that followed them, and that rock was Christ. **1 Corinthians 10:4**

❧❧❧

Spiritual: (PNEUMATIKOS' πνευματικός) *adj.*
pneumatic, supernatural

Another Picture of Christ

There is a fountain located inside this solid outcropping of natural bedrock which dates back more than 1,000 years before Christ. We don't know how, but sometime back then the people living in this area discovered that there was water coming out of this rock. So, they chiseled away at it until they had carved an entrance to walk inside.

Later, during the 1st millennium BC, this fountain took on sacred significance when it became identified with popular legends in Corinth, especially that of Jason and Medea. According to this story, Jason and his wife Medea settled in Corinth and established a family there. At one point, Jason fell in love with Glauke, a local princess, the daughter of the king, and left Medea for her.

Medea became furious with Jason and revenged her scorn by gifting Glauke with a poisoned dress. When Glauke put this garment on, it stuck to her and then burst into flames. To extinguish the fire, Glauke jumped into this fountain to her death.

Based on this legend, the Corinthians named the fountain after her and soon four sanctuaries were built around it—temples to Apollo, Hera, Athena and Zeus Almighty. As needs arose, local people would frequent this "sacred" rock to draw "blessed" water from it.

During the time when the Apostle Paul stayed in Corinth, he would have passed by "the Glauke fountain" many times and observed people trying to quench their thirst with this *special* water.

This may be the reason why Paul used the language of drinking a *spiritual* drink from a *spiritual* rock when he wrote to the Corinthians about finding their *spiritual* supply in Christ (1 Cor 10:4) as he connected this rock fountain to another one found in Exodus 17:1-7. When Moses struck that rock, water flowed out of it too.

That Exodus event is only referenced once in the New Testament. Do you think it's a coincidence that it's in this letter? Paul seems to say, O Corinthians, there is different rock that can take away your spiritual thirst—and that rock is Christ!

The Trophy

He (undressed) the principalities and powers… and disgraced them in public by **triumphing over** them (by the cross).

Colossians 2:15

⁂

Triumphing over: (THRIAMBEU'O θριαμβεύω) *v.* celebrating the victory after the battle

A Symbol of Christ's Triumphant Victory

There is a special artifact in the Archaeological Museum at Corinth that I would like to show you. It is the breastplate on a statue of a man. In the center of this breastplate is a trophy. But what is a trophy?

A trophy was a wooden pole that a soldier found on a battlefield upon which he fixed the spoils taken from his defeated foe. A victorious warrior would completely undress and disarm his dead enemy and hang his clothing and weapons on this pole as a symbol of victory.

Then, as he returned from battle, this warrior would join others marching home in a triumphant spectacle, holding their trophies high, banners of their conquest, for all to see.

The Apostle Paul used this spectacular trophy imagery to describe Christ's triumphant victory over his enemies by the cross (Col 2:15). There, on a wooden pole, Jesus disarmed and undressed the powers of the evil spiritual world, leaving them naked and without weapons.

Jesus also used "trophy" language to illustrate his power over Satan, saying to his disciples, "When the strong man (Satan), fully armed, guards his own palace, his goods are secure; but when one stronger that he (Jesus) attacks him and overpowers him, he takes away his armor (his demonic powers) in which he has placed his trust and divides up his spoil" (Luke 11:21-22).

In this parable in Luke, what are his goods and his spoils? And what are the trophies and weapons captured by Christ in Col 2:15?

We are.

When Adam and Eve turned their backs on God, we human beings surrendered ourselves to Satan's control and became his goods. And for generations people have been the weapons used by the evil powers to maintain their satanic dominion of the earth... until Jesus came.

When Jesus defeated his foes on the cross, he freed human beings by taking us, the spoils of his victory, out from under the power of evil. People, the tools that once were used by Satan for evil, now became the righteous tools God uses for good.

Sailing from Cenchrea

I commend to you our sister Phoebe, who is a **servant** of the church in Cenchrea, so that you may receive her in the Lord in a manner worthy of the saints, and give her any help she may need from you; for she has been of great assistance to many, including myself. **Romans 16:1-2**

❧❧❧

Servant: (DIAK'ONOS διάκοηος) *n.*
deaconess, someone who ministers to others

Paul's Journey Ends in Phoebe's Town

Paul stayed in Corinth over 18 months before deciding that it was time to return home to Antioch. He had been gone a long time. So, saying farewell to the brothers and with his co-workers Priscilla and Aquila, he boarded a ship bound for Syria from the port city of Cenchrea.

Corinth, located on narrow isthmus between two seas, had two seaports—the port of Lachaeum, five miles to the north from which ships traveled west to Italy, and Cenchrea, seven miles east of the city, a port that served Asia Minor and the eastern Mediterranean.

According to Romans 16, there was a church in Cenchrea, possibly established during Paul's stay in Corinth. It was the home church of a woman named Phoebe, who the Bible calls a deaconess.

In those days, a deaconess was a *servant* of the church, a Christian sister who served the believers by doing various charitable works. These activities might include visiting the sick, helping the poor, mentoring younger women or providing hospitality to travelers.

In Rom 16:1-2, Paul introduces Phoebe to his Roman readers and says that she "has been of *great assistance* to many." This probably means that she was "a patroness," an influential person of status and wealth who may have provided aid to the downtrodden and despised.

In these verses, Paul says that Phoebe is about to embark on a trip to their city. Most likely, she will carry this letter to the church with her. What makes this odd is that in antiquity, ladies rarely traveled, and they didn't take long trips alone.

We don't know what serious business took Phoebe to Rome. But we do know that Paul commended her to the Christians there and asked them to help her in any way they could.

As Paul's European ministry began with an encounter with Lydia, a lady in Philippi, a small town *near* a seaport, it seems only fitting that his journey would end in similar fashion, with thoughts of Phoebe, a lady, from Cenchrea, a small town *with* a seaport.

Notes

7 *Plato and Aristotle:* Conybeare, *Life & Epistles*, Vol 1, 366.

9 *The divine light:* From a lecture given by C.S. Lewis to the Oxford Socratic Club on Nov 6, 1944. Lewis, *Is Theology Poetry?*, 8-9.

The Ancient World

17 *the Creator declared himself:* "The heavens proclaim the glory of God. The skies display his craftsmanship. Day after day they continue to speak; night after night they make him known." Psalm 19:1-2 NLT.

17 *all human beings, regardless of their origins, can find God:* "Theology, while saying that a special illumination has been vouchsafed to Christians and (earlier) to Jews, also says that there is some divine illumination vouchsafed to all men." Lewis, *Is Theology Poetry?*, 8.

17 *chaff to be burned:* "Strict Jews believed that God had no use for the Gentiles." Barclay, *Acts*, 93, 125. Also, "There is no opinion of the Jews more conspicuous in the sacred writings, than that they were greatly superior to the Gentiles; that the theocracy and all its blessings belonged to them; and that others could attain even an inferior station in the kingdom of the Messiah only by becoming Jews." Hodge, *Romans*, 8.

19 *While Israel knew God's presence directly:* Richardson, *Eternity*, 23-29.

19 *indirectly through nature:* "This knowledge of God is independent... of such a special revelation as had been given to the Jews... God's power and the totality of the Divine nature, are inevitably impressed on the mind by nature." Denney, *Romans*, 592.

19 *labor and discovery are required:* "The Greek ideal," says Frederic Godet, "... is a masterpiece of wisdom... this people, with their inquisitive and subtle mind, would get at the essence of things." Godet, *First Corinthians*, 104-105.

21 *King-priests (wanax in Greek)*: Palaima, Thomas (1992, December). *The Nature of the Mycenaean Wanax: Non-Indo-European Origins of Priestly Functions.* [Paper presentation]. In Rehak, ed., *The Role of the Ruler in the Prehistoric Aegean.* Annual Meeting of the Archaeological Institute of America, New Orleans (pp. 119-139).

21 *the Myceneans that came after them:* : Crielaard, Jan Paul (2007, June). *The 'Wanax to Basileus Model' Reconsidered.* [Paper presentation]. In Ainian, Alexander, ed., *The "Dark Ages" Revisited.* Acts of an International Symposium in Memory of William D.E. Coulson, Volos. University of Thessaly Press, 2011 (pp. 83-111).

21 *This unique person:* "Historically, Melchizedek appears to have belonged to a dynasty of priest-kings in which he had both predecessors and successors." Bruce, *Hebrews*, 137.

21 *Melchizedek blessed Abram:* Abram met another Gentile king, Abimelech, king of the Philistines (Gen 21:32). Like the Minoans, the Philistines came from the island of Crete (called, Caphtor). Jer 47:4; Amos 9:7. This means that Abimelech was also a king-priest.

21 *Melchizedek pre-figures Jesus Christ:* "a throned Priest-King." Swete, *The Ascended Christ*, 95.

23 *Cliesthenes:* Plutarch, the famous 1st century Greek biographer and philosopher, refers to Cleisthenes in his biographies of Themistocles and Pericles in his work, known as *Parallel Lives*.

23 *This novel political/social system:* Aristotle, the 4th century BC Greek philosopher, from *Athenian Republic*, 21.1.1 – 22.8.1.

23 *"the measure of all things":* Protagoras of Abdera, a famous 5th century BC Greek thinker, made this phrase proverbial. Plato restated this quotation in one of his Dialogues, *Theaetetus*, 152a.

25 *"the Decapolis":* "The names of the ten cities were Damascus, Philadelphia, Raphana, Scythopolis, Gadara, Hippos, Dion, Pella, Gerasa and Canatha." Edersheim, *The Life and Times of Jesus*, 87.

25 *in walking distance of Jesus' home:* "About an hour's walk away." Singer, *Jewish Encyclopedia*, 198-199.

25 *he left behind a completely new world:* "His empire, as a political unity, did not survive his death in 323 BC; but the cultural empire which he founded lasted for a thousand years." Bruce, *New Testament History*, 2.

27 *the Jews also knew Greek:* Kittel, *Dictionary*, Vol. II, 506.

27 *Jesus...would have been fluent in Greek:* "Jesus, who lived only in Palestine, needed no interpreter but himself spoke Greek to Pilate." Lenski, *Acts*, 240.

27 *All...were written in Greek:* As NT Greek scholar Bruce Metzger says, "The authors of almost all of the books of the New Testament were Jews... all of them wrote in Greek." Metzger, *Language*, 46.

Philippi

37 *"man of Macedonia":* "This 'man' has been variously interpreted by Bible commentators as referring to Luke, Lydia or 'the cry of Europe for Christ.'" Robertson, *Word Pictures*, Vol. III, 248.

39 *famous ship builders:* Thirlwall, *History of Greece*, 72.

41 *four smaller districts:* "Macedonia was unusual as a Roman province in being divided into four subprovinces, of which Philippi belonged to the first… it's capital city was Amphipolis." Marshall, *Acts*, 266.

41 *a miniature Rome:* The 2nd century Roman writer Aulus Gellius says that Philippi was "a portrait of the mother city on a small scale." Jamieson, *Commentary*, 359.

41 *the first district of Macedonia:* "And this epithet of first would belong to it not only as regarding the journey of Paul and Silas, but as lying furthest eastward, for which reason also the district was called Macedonia prima." Alford, *New Testament*, Vol. 1, 760.

43 *the stream Krenides:* Fant, *Guide*, 110.

43 *Lydia, a businesswoman:* A. J. Maclean, *Hastings Dictionary*, 560.

43 *the dyeing process:* "The purple dye was obtained from a conchylium, the shellfish Murex trunculus of Linneaus, and the waters of Thyatira produced the brightest and most permanent hues." Lenski, *Acts*, 656.

45 *a school for adults:* Around 350 BC, Aristotle wrote a book called *Poetics* which analyzed the classical drama, specifically the tragedy. Ancient drama was always presented in poetic form with music, like our operas. Dramatists were included in lists of poets. *Poetics* contains exceptional insights into the use of theaters as schools for adults in the Athenian society during classical times.

47 *more than a marketplace:* "Marketplace conveys a very inadequate idea of the Greek agora. The agora was an open space in the centre of the city which served as the focus of civic life. Around it were grouped the public buildings of the city, the temples of its patron gods, its senate-house, town-hall and law courts." Rackham, *Acts*, 309.

49 *But the bema:* "This word means step, orator's platform, and then a platform or raised dais for the seat of the judge." Lenski, *Acts*, 755.

51 *they were actually taken two places:* "The city-judges (*archontas*) must have referred the matter to the *strategoi*." Meyer, *Acts*, 314.

53 *tradition has claimed:* Pelekanidou, *Traditional Prison*, 427-435.

53 *But recent research:* Hellenic Ministry of Culture, *St Paul's Prison*, 35.

53 *There is no logical reason:* Fant, *Guide*, 108.

53 *housing for the jailor and his family above:* Mounce's Greek Interlinear translates Acts 16:34: "And when he had brought them *up* into his house." Mounce, *Greek New Testament*, 529. Also, Meyer, "We are to think of the official dwelling of the jailer as being built *above* the prison cells." Meyer, *Acts*, 317.

55 *while under ecstatic trances:* The English word *ecstasy* is a transliteration of the Greek work *ekstasis*, literally, (*ek* out of, *stasis* a standing). *Ekstatis* is a displacement "in which a person is so transported out of his natural state that he falls into a trance." Vine, *Dictionary*, 44.

55 *"a way of salvation":* "A way of salvation, strictly speaking (no article). There were many 'ways of salvation' offered to men then as now." Robertson, *Word Pictures*, Vol. III, 255.

57 *Religious syncretism:* "... the tendency within Hellenistic religion to identify the deities of different peoples and to fuse their cults." Rowdon, *International Bible Commentary*, 1048.

57 *they demanded it:* "Emperor worship was a way for Roman leaders to establish their power (and loyalty to the Emperor) in the Eastern Mediterranean." Jeffers, *Greco-Roman World*, 101.

57 *"Jesus is Lord!":* "No Gentile would do this who had not ceased worshipping the emperor as Kurios." Robertson, *Word Pictures*, Vol. IV, 389.

59 *the octagon church:* "This chapel...was dedicated to the Apostle Paul. A mosaic inscription found here reads: 'Porphyrios, bishop, made the embroidery (a mosaic floor) of the basilica of Paul in Christ.'" Fant, *Guide*, 106.

59 *the equal value of the many different parts:* Paul speaks at length of the function and value of the members of Christ's body in his second letter to the Corinthians (2 Cor 12:12-27).

59 *the religion of the state:* Schaff, *History*, Vol. 3, 389.

Thessalonica

65 *left their co-workers:* Meyer, *Acts*, 319.

65 *Amphipolis and Apollonia:* "The stops here mentioned are thus particularized in the itineraries: Philippi to Amphipolis, 37 miles: Amphipolis to Apollonia, 30 miles: Apollonia to Thessalonica, 37 miles." Alford, *New Testament*, Vol. 1, 765.

65 *connect Rome with the provinces:* Conybeare, *Life*, Vol. I, 316.

65 *15 feet deep:* "The Roman roads were notable for their straightness, solid foundations, cambered surfaces facilitating drainage, and the use of concrete." Britannica. *Roman Road System*.

65 *greatly facilitated travel:* Most of the time. "During the Roman period, popular use of the road made its traffic so heavy that Cicero once delayed his departure from Thessalonica (July, 57 BC) because of 'the constant traffic' on it." Fant, *Guide*, 11.

67 *politarches:* "Politarches was the correct title for the native magistrates of a free Macedonian city. The word was previously unknown and quoted against Luke's accuracy." Macgregor, *Acts*, 228.

67 *not found anywhere in Greek literature:* Furneaux, *Acts*, 275.

69 *offer their victories back to the gods:* Kittel, *Dictionary*, Vol. VII, 620.

69 *"to bind around":* Abbott-Smith, *Lexicon*, 106.

71 *woven from branches:* Kittel, *Dictionary*, Vol. VII, 616-617.

71 *Great prestige came to the winners:* "They suffer and do all this (training) to attain a wreath of olive-leaves or ivy and to be proclaimed victor by the herald." Kittel, *Dictionary*, Vol. VII, 620.

71 *woven headpieces became a popular thing:* Kittel, *Dictionary*, Vol. VII, 621-622.

73 *Another priceless artifact:* The golden wreaths in the Thessalonica Museum are not identified. But the three golden wreaths in the Vergina Museum are identified: King Philip's (oak), the royal wife's (myrtle) and a teenager who may be Alexander IV (oak).

73 *the word for a royal crown (stemma) is not mentioned at all:* In the Gospels, the so-called "crown of thorns" that the Romans placed on Jesus' head was actually a "wreath *(stephanos)* of thorns." They did this to mock him: "Instead of a winner, you are a loser!" (Matt 27:27-31).

73 *to honor their patron god:* Kittel, *Dictionary*, Vol. VII, 616.

Berea

77 *a Jewish institution:* A.R.S. Kennedy, *Hastings Dictionary*, 882-884.

77 *"living water":* "The 'living,' i.e. 'flowing' water of the spring is greatly preferred to the 'dead' water of the cistern, and frequently it stands for the vitalizing influences of God's grace" (John 7:37-38; Jer 2:13; Zech 14:3). W. Ewing, *Hastings Dictionary*, 966.

79 *this special scroll:* Antonoglu, *Ancient scroll*, 28-31.

Vergina

83 *a boatman:* Charon, the ferryman, rows a boat that carries the dead across the river Acheron, the border between the upper and lower worlds. Pausanias, *Book 10*, 28. See also Aristophanes, *Frogs*, 152-188, and Lucian's *Dialogues of the Dead*.

83 *from which there is no return:* Hesiod describes a dreadful dog, Cerberus, who guards Hades' entrance and "devours whomever he catches going out the Gates." Hesiod, *Theogony*, 767-774.

83 *Jesus uses many of these Greek terms:* "In conforming himself to the ordinary language current on these subjects, it is to suppose that He, whose essence is Truth, could have assumed as existing anything that does not exist." Alford, *New Testament,* Vol. I, 402.

83 *both parts of Hades:* Vincent gives an extensive discussion of Hades in his Notes on Matt 16:18. Vincent, *Word Studies*, Vol. I, 93-96.

85 *"Abraham's side":* "A rabbinical phrase, equivalent to being with Abraham in Paradise." Vincent, *Word Studies*, Vol. I, 398.

85 *"the isles of the blessed":* Kittel, *Dictionary*, Vol. IV, 362.

85 *primarily used in connection with the gods:* "let them be witnesses by the blessed (*makarios*) gods." Homer, *Iliad,* 1:339. "but bid her swear a great oath by the blessed (*makarios*) gods." Homer, *Odyessy,* 10:229.

85 *Paul:* In 1 Timothy, Paul used *makarios* in the way the Greeks did: "the gospel of the glory of the blessed (*makarios*) God" (1 Tim 1:11); and, "To the blessed (*makarios*) and only Sovereign" (1 Tim 6:15).

87 *son of the Greek god Apollo:* "I begin to sing of Asclepius, son of Apollo and healer of sicknesses." Homer, *Homeric Hymns*, 16.1.

87 *heal people:* "(Asclepius) who drove pain from the limbs that he healed, that hero who cured all types of diseases." Pindar, *Pythian Hymn #13*, 4-7. Also, "our forefather Asclepius composed this science of ours." Plato, *Symposium*, 186.

89 *There, he may have visited the Old Testament saints:* "Some of the Fathers, as Irenaeus, Tertullian… Calvin …regard the spirits in prison as the spirits of the just, especially of the Old Testament saints." Alford, *New Testament*, Vol. II, Part II, 815.

Meteora

93 *Anthony from Alexandria:* Schaff, *History*, Vol. 3, 181-189.

93 *wilderness:* "For Jesus the 'place without inhabitants' is one where nothing separates him from God and which he therefore seeks when he wants to escape the crowds… What he primarily seeks there is the stillness of prayer." Kittel, *Dictionary*, Vol. II, 658.

95 *Benedictus:* Schaff, *History*, Vol. 3, 216-226.

97 *like a potter with clay:* "God is pictured as a potter. He forms man from the dust." Elwell, *Baker Commentary*, 12.

97 *Paul gave a command… to work with their hands:* "Paul gave a new dignity to manual labor by precept and example." Robertson, *Word Pictures*, Vol. IV, 30.

99 *the "iconoclastic controversy":* Schaff, *History*, Vol. 4, 454-474.

Delphi

101 *at the center of the Greek world:* "(Apollo's temple) was also supposed to be the center of the habitable earth and was called the Navel of the Earth." Strabo, *Geography*, 9.3.6.

105 *Coretas:* "The power hovering about this spot was first made manifest when a certain shepherd fell in by accident and gave inspired utterance... his name... was Coretas." Plutarch. *Περί των Έκλελοιπότων Χρηστηρίων*, 433, C-D, 42.

105 *where priestesses delivered Apollo's guidance:* "Apollo's oracle has tamed the darker side of the cosmos... it therefore gives men divine guidance through which they can cope with this side of the cosmos." Hornblower, *Oxford*, 445.

107 *Both buildings had two rooms:* The writer of Hebrews describes the two-room design of the Old Testament Tabernacle in Heb 9:2-3. The temple in Jerusalem had a similar two-room design. A.R.S. Kennedy, *Hastings Dictionary*, 904.

107 *inhale the intoxicating vapors:* Strabo, *Geography*, 9.3.5.

109 *When Greek prophetes were dispatched:* In classical Greek literature there are four terms that have similar yet different meanings and are often confused in English translations. 1) *Prophetes*: preannouncer; 2) *Keryx*: herald, public messenger; 3) *Aggelos*: emissary, private messenger (angel); and 4) *Mantis*: diviner, soothsayer.

109 *called kerykeion in Greek:* In Homer it is also called a scepter. Homer, *Iliad*, 24.339 ff and *Odyssey*, 5.28 ff.

111 *early Christian apologists:* "Both Theophilus of Antioch and Clement of Alexandria, 2nd century Christian theologians, referred to the Sibyl as a prophetess apparently no less inspired than the Old Testament prophets." Britannica. *Sibylline Oracles.*

111 *the continuous wait:* MVSEI VATACANI, *Sybils and Prophets*, 1.

111 *all mankind:* "Theophilus unapologetically and clearly makes the Sibyl a prophetess with a validity and inspiration equal to that of the Biblical prophets... The Sibyl is distinguished from the Biblical prophets only by the fact that she was active among the Greeks rather than the Hebrews." Hooker, *Sybils*, 162,165.

113 *spoke to strength, discipline:* Bond, *Olympic Nudity*, 6.

113 *Jews were prohibited from participating:* "Conservative Jews continued to rail against athletic nudity... nudity was forbidden." McDonnel, *Athletic Nudity*, 405.

113 *Yet in his letters:* "The Apostle often uses language drawn from these (games)." Conybeare, *Life*, Vol. II, 198-200.

115 *a gymnasium... Jerusalem:* According to 2 Maccabees 4:7-14, when the Seleucid king, Antiochus Epiphanes, came to power, Jason, the Jewish high priest, built a gymnasium in Jerusalem and encouraged the youth to take part in discus throwing and in the "unlawful exercises on the athletic fields." NAB, 668.

115 *Not a weight. But a garment:* Like laying off old clothes (Col 3:8). "(Laying off) every encumbrance that handicaps... no trailing garment to hinder or trip on." Robertson, *Word Pictures*, Vol. V, 432.

117 *the most exciting and prestigious:* Conybeare, *Life*, Vol. II, 198.

117 *a distance of one stadia:* Abbot-Smith, *Lexicon*, 415.

117 *fixing our gaze upon Jesus:* "on whom faith depends from start to finish." Bruce, *Hebrews*, 351.

119 *Gallio, a noble Roman:* Longnecker, *Acts*, 485.

119 *The Gallio inscription:* Murphy-O'Connor, *St. Paul's Corinth*, 161.

121 *to commemorate a victory:* Washburn, *Charioteer of Delphi*, 153.

121 *Apollo was the god of culture and music:* Hornblower, *Oxford*, 122.

Athens

124 *Pireaus:* This primary port of Athens was joined to the ancient city by walls (pictured on this map), that were 6 kilometers long, to provide a safe means of escape for residents should attacks come by land.

127 *Lady Wisdom:* "I begin to sing of Pallas Athena, the glorious goddess, bright-eyed, inventive, unbending of heart, pure virgin, savior of cities, courageous, Tritogeneia." Homer, *Homeric Hymns*, 28.1.

127 *This massive marble temple:* Hornblower, *Oxford*, 1116.

129 *out jumped Athena:* "Wise Zeus bare her from his sacred head, arrayed in warlike arms of flashing gold, and awe seized all the gods as they gazed. But Athena sprang quickly from the immortal head and stood before Zeus." Homer, *Homeric Hymns #28.*

129 *Proverbs 8:22-31 where Christ is pictured*: Hodgkin, *Christ in All*, 121.

129 *the eternal Son of God, is the agent of creation:* Westcott, *St. John*, 4.

131 *imagining their gods in human form:* "A highly distinctive feature of the early Greek idea of God is anthropomorphism. The gods have for the most part human qualities, emotions and customs. Above all, they have human form." Kittel, *Dictionary*, Vol. III, 71. In Romans 1:23, Paul speaks of two categories of idols, those which look like humans and those which look like animals. "The worship of man,"

says Frederic Godet, "especially characterized Greek and Roman Polytheism; that of the different classes of animals, Egyptian and Barbarian paganism." Godet, *Romans*, 106.

131 *Pillars began to look like people:* The illustration on page 130 is "the porch of the maidens" on a building called the Erechtheion at the Acropolis of Athens.

133 *Romulus and Remus:* "According to the mythology, Mars was the father of these children (who later founded Rome)." Strabo, *Geography*, 5.3.2.

133 *she conquered us with her culture:* Horace, *Book 2, Epistle 1*, 156.

135 *Cleisthenes was the first person:* "(He) restored the body of the people to power, expelled the tyrants and established that Democracy to which the world of Hellas (Greece) owes its greatest blessings." Isocrates, *Αρεοπαγιτικός*, 7.16-17.

135 *the living body:* In Greek there are two synonymous terms for the English term *body*: the older one, mostly used by Homer (*demas*) and the one used by most of the classics and the New Testament (*soma*).

137 *"outsiders" (idiotes):* "Our ordinary citizens, though occupied with the pursuits of industry, are still fair judges of public matters; for, unlike any other nation, regarding him who takes no part in these duties, keeping himself private (*idiotes*), not as unambitious but as useless, we Athenians are able to judge..." Thucydides, *The History, Book II*, 40:1-13.

139 *This six-minute speech:* Still today in the common Greek vernacular the term *logos* carries a wide variety of meanings, including all of the five required elements of an ancient Athenian speech.

141 *kleros:* "All of the officials concerned with the regular administration are appointed by lot (*kleros*)." Aristotle, *Athenian Constitution*, 63-64.

141 *cheirotoneo:* "The Treasurer of Military Funds... all military officers are elected by a show of hands." Aristotle, *Athenian Constitution*, 43.1.1-7.

143 *confined there for ten years:* Hornblower, *Oxford*, 1083.

143 *ostracon:* "The method of procedure—to give a general outline—was as follows: Each voter took an *ostracon* and wrote the name of that citizen whom he wished to remove from the city." Plutarch, *Aristides*, 7:4-6.

145 *(ekklesia), came from Athens:* "The *ekklesia* was the lawful assembly in a free Greek city of all those possessed of the rights of citizenship, for the transaction of public affairs. That they were *summoned* is expressed

in the latter part of the word... that they were summoned out of the whole population… is expressed in the first." Trench, *Synonyms*, 2.

145 *both locally and universally:* "(a) The whole company of believers throughout the present era, and (b) in a singular number to a company of professed believers." Vine, *Dictionary*, 76.

147 *a "Great Mind" must have created nature:* Speaking of the ancient Greek thinkers, the 1st century Jewish philosopher Philo wrote: "Admiring and being struck with amazement at (the order and beauty of Nature), they arrived at a conception consistent with what they had seen, that all these beauties so admirable in their arrangement have not come into being spontaneously, but are the work of some Maker, the Creator of the world." Sanday, *Romans*, 43.

149 *including human sins and imperfections:* "(Paul) saw that idolatry and license went together. He knew that the heathen myths about their gods ascribed to them all manner of immoralities." Sanday, *Romans*, 49. "Xenophanes attacks Homer and Hesiod for portraying the gods as behaving in ways that are blameworthy for mortals." Hornblower, *Oxford*, 1628.

149 *he called this real One, "the Being.":* This identical title for God appears in Exodus 3:14 in the Septuagint, a version of the Hebrew Scriptures translated into Greek by Jewish interpreters in the 3rd century BC. "And God spoke to Moses, saying, I am THE BEING… say to the children of Israel, THE BEING has sent me to you." Through discovery, Parmenides had arrived at the same realization of who God is that God had spoken directly to Moses a thousand years earlier. Brenton, *Septuagint*, 73.

149 *the way, the truth and the life:* Parmenides, *On Nature*, Simplicius, *Caption to Aristotle's* "**Περί Ουρανού**," 557.20.28-30 and Simplicius, *Caption to Aristotle's* "**Φυσικήν Ακρόασιν**," 179.31.8.1-6.

151 *that I know nothing!:* Plato, *Apology*, 21a-e.

151 *Socrates… search for "the good":* Plato, *Apology*, 21a-e.

153 *Euclides linked Socrate's ideas of the agathos:* "Euclides of Megara: God = Phronesis = The Good." Drozdek, *Acta Antigua*, 27-34.

155 *The Stoics were descendants of Plato, Socrates and others:* Zeno, who was the founder of Stoicism, taught in the Stoa Poecile (Painted Stoa) in Athens, which gave its name to Stoicism. Longnecker, *Acts*, 474.

155 *"let us eat, drink and be merry":* Also found in the Old Testament. "Let us eat and drink; for tomorrow, we shall die." Isa 22:13. KJV

157 *Ares…put on trial for the murder of Poseidon's son:* Fant, *Guide*, 24.

157 *the Supreme Court of Athens:* Even today in Greece, the Supreme Court, the place where serious crimes or appeals are brought, is commonly known as the Mars Hill Court.

159 *Stoas...were public gathering places:* "The primary function of the stoa was to provide shelter for large numbers of people." Thompson, *Stoa*, 3.

159 *Herod...was a fanatic Hellenist:* Josephus, *Complete Works, Antiquities*, XV, XI. Also, "Despite (Herod's) apparent dedication to the Abrahamic faith in renovating the Temple Mount, Herod was a committed Hellenist." ben Zion, *Herod.*

161 *quoting two Greek poets:* In Acts 17:28, Paul quotes two Greek poets. "On two other occasions Paul quotes from Greek poets. He quotes Meander in 1 Cor 15:33 and... from Epimenides... in Titus 1:12." Lenski, *Acts*, 733.

163 *stay close to the athletic venues:* The Isthmian Games were held at the sanctuary of Poseidon on the isthmus of Corinth (from which they received their name). This site was some five kilometers from the city.

163 *Paul arrived in Corinth shortly before Gallio was named proconsul:* "So (Paul) stayed (in Corinth) a year and six months, teaching among them the word of God. But when Gallio was proconsul of Achaia, the Jews rose up..." Acts 18:11-12.

Eleusis

167 *Participants included some Roman Emperors:* Octavian Augustus, Hadrian, Marcus Aurelias, Antoninus Pius and others. The mysteries in Eleusis "had been elevated to be the state cult of Athens and recognized by the Roman Empire." Kittel, *Dictionary*, Vol. IV, 808.

167 *We know that Jesus knew about "the mysteries:"* We know this by the specific terminology he used and the structure of these technical terms.

167 *those who were initiated into his heavenly kingdom:* "The secret is no longer hidden from the initiated. Discipleship means initiation into the secret of God's kingdom." Robertson, *Word Pictures*, Vol. 1, 285.

169 *a temple built in the 5th century:* The name of this temple of Demeter and Persephone was the Eleusinion. It was located on the north slope of the Acropolis.

169 *purification ceremonies with fastings, washing in the sea:* These and other details about the mysteries of Eleusis can be found in a book published in 1909 by the German archeologist, Otto Kern, *Eleusinische Beiträge*, (Eleusian Contributions).

171 *A revelation is an apokalypsis:* "(Jesus) is the corporeal revelation of God, though at first concealed as everything divine is in this age." Kittel, *Dictionary*, Vol. III, 580.

171 *Paul used the word mystery:* "The etymology of the Greek word for 'mystery' is itself a mystery. Probable, but not certain, its derivation comes from *muein*, 'to close.'" Kittel, *Dictionary*, Vol. IV, 803.

173 *According to this myth:* The myth of Demeter and Persephone came from a collection of poems once attributed to Homer: "To Demeter." Evelyn-White, *Hesiod*, 289-325.

173 *wheat soon became...the symbol of the mysteries:* Since Demeter was the goddess of harvest, images of her often contain sheafs of wheat.

Corinth

179 *they destroyed most of the city:* Because the Romans honored Greek religion, they left some of the temples in Corinth standing. According to British geographer and historian W.M. Leake, "The site (of ancient Corinth), I conceive, cannot have been quite uninhabited, as the Romans neither destroyed the public buildings nor persecuted the religion of the Corinthians. As many of those buildings were still perfect in the time of Pausanias, there must have been some persons who had the care of them during the century of desolation." Leake, *Travels*, III, 231, Note a.

179 *housed over 1,000 female temple slaves:* Strabo was a Greek geographer and historian who was a contemporary of the Apostle Paul. They may have been in Corinth during the same time. Strabo wrote that "the temple of Aphrodite was so rich that it owned more than a thousand temple slaves, courtesans, whom both men and women had dedicated to the goddess. And therefore it was also on account of these women that the city was crowded with people and grew rich." Strabo, *Geography*, 8.6.20.

179 *practiced sacred prostitution:* Archaeological evidence uncovered in Corinth proves that "the preexisting Olympian cults continued to function after the refounding (of Corinth by the Romans)... this continuity can be seen in the resumption of the worship of Aphrodite on Acrocorinth." Bookidis, *Sanctuaries*, 257. In his warning to the Corinthian church (1 Cor 6:15-20), the fact that Paul connects prostitutes, fornication, temples, slavery and ransom together in one passage, strongly suggests that sacred prostitution was still being practiced in Corinth at his time. To this end, G.G. Findlay in his commentary on 1 Corinthians connects this passage with the temple of Aphrodite. Findlay, *1 Corinthian*s, 819-822. See also F.F. Bruce, *New Testament History*, 314.

179 *To "Corinthianize" meant to practice sex with abandon:* "To live as the Corinthians do was a euphemism for the vilest kind of life." Tenney, *New Testament Survey*, 288.

181 *They shaved their heads:* This practice of shaming women by shaving their heads has continued through the centuries up until today.

181 *French women… had their heads shaved:* "As we mark the 65th anniversary of the D-day landings, Anthony Beevor describes a dark side to the liberation parties (in France)." Beevor, *An Ugly Carnival.*

181 *completely cover:* This unique Greek word *katakalypto* is only used one time in the New Testament (1 Cor 11:5). Here it means that none of a woman's hair should be showing at all. This same word is used in the Greek Old Testament (Septuagint) in Exodus 26:31 "in the command that Moses should place the ark within the holy of holies and hide it from sight behind a curtain." Kittel, *Dictionary*, Vol. III, 561.

183 *the "higher critics":* "Their 'new theology' stands… for the denial or questioning of the Bible as the inerrant Word of God… of the real deity of our Lord and Savior Jesus Christ… of the virgin birth… of the resurrection…" Torrey, *Higher Criticism*, 5-6.

183 *a city treasurer…held a high office:* This was a common practice across the Roman world.

185 *we are speaking about redeeming slaves:* The practice of slave redemption was widespread among the Romans. Deissmann, *Light*, 321-330.

187 *these emancipated females:* These independent women, through the help of wealthy men, "could exert (their) own influence and obtain (their) own great wealth." Hornblower, *Oxford*, 702.

187 *"it is improper for a woman to speak in church":* Paul used a unique Greek word for "speak" here (*laleo*). In those days, when this word was used to describe adult speech it was usually a sign of scorn and meant "to prattle or babble" as opposed to rational normal speech. Kittel, *Dictionary*, Vol. IV, 76.

189 *as he embraced this pillar, he was flogged:* This method of scourging was "endured by Christ and administered by the order of Pilate." Vine, *Expository Dictionary*, 999. See Matt 27:26 and Mark 15:15.

191 *Antiochus Epiphanes…built a Greek gymnasium:* See note on page 115.

193 *the Peirene Fountain:* "Pierene was a woman who was turned into a spring of water by the tears she shed in bewailing her son Cenchrias who Artemis had unwittingly killed." Pausanias, *Description of Greece*, II, 3, 2 (J.G. Fraser's translation).

195 *"participants of the altar":* This title was common in the religious practices across the whole Mediterranean world and extended even to the Jews as 1 Cor 10:18 suggests.

195 *enjoy low cost meat:* "In the Macellum at Pompei we could imagine to ourselves the poor Christians buying their modest pound of meat in the Corinth Macellum (1 Cor 10:25)." Deissmann, *Light*, 276.

195 *but let your conscience:* Godet, *First Corinthians*, 522-523.

195 *found during an excavation in 1898:* Cadbury, *Macellum*, 134.

197 *Medea became furious...and revenged her scorn:* Euripides tells this story in his play *Medea* where he describes the conflict Medea feels as a mother and a betrayed wife. Medea, in her monologue, says in effect, "I know what is good to do, but I am bound by the evil." This is very similar to what Paul says in Rom 7:19-21.

199 *trophy:* "A token of the enemy's rout, consisting of shields, helmets, etc., hung on trees or fixed on upright posts." Liddel, *Lexicon*, 717.

199 *Christ's triumphant victory:* Vine comments on the phrase in Col 2:15, "having spoiled principalities and powers" in the KJV Bible: "There is no doubt that Satan and his hosts gathered together to attack the soul of Christ, while he was enduring, in propitiatory sacrifice, the judgment due to our sins... (This) seems to stand simply as a vivid description of (Christ's) repulsion of their attack and of the power by which he completely overthrew them." Vine, *Dictionary*, 1080.

199 *In Luke, what are his goods and his spoils?:* "The strong man is the adversary, Satan; his palace is this present world (John 12:31; 14:30; 16:11). His goods, or tools, or spoils are the sons of men (2 Tim 2:26; 1 John 5:19)." Alford, *New Testament*, Vol. I, 366.

201 *Paul introduces Phoebe:* Frederic Godet describes Phoebe as "a rich and devoted woman." Godet, *Romans*, 488.

201 *"a patroness":* "There were so many services to be rendered to the poor, to orphans, to strangers, to the sick, which women only could render." Godet, *Romans*, 488. "The word... means a benefactor: it is a high and honorable title." Hodge, *Romans*, 448.

201 *she will carry this letter:* "Phoebe was clearly a person of substance and leadership. She was almost certainly going to Rome on business on her own account, and it is a matter of great significance that it is to her that Paul entrusts the delivery of this, his fullest and most remarkable letter." Wright, *Romans*, 135.

Bibliography

Abbott-Smith, G. *A Manual Greek Lexicon of the New Testament.* Edinburgh: T.&T. Clark, 1937.

Alford, Henry. *The New Testament for English Readers.* London: Rivingtons, 1863.

Antonoglou, Eleanna. *An ancient scroll found in the Veria Synagogue: History and Life of the Jewish Community of Veria.* Athens: Central Board of Jewish Communities in Greece, 2002.

Aristotle. *Athenian Constitution.* 4th century BC.

Aristotle. *Athenian Republic.* 4th century BC.

Aristotle. *Poetics.* 4th century BC.

Barclay, William. *The Acts of the Apostles.* Louisville: Westminster John Knox Press, 1975.

Beevor, Anthony. "*An Ugly Carnival*" (online). London: The Guardian, 4 Jun 2009. Accessed Feb 8, 2021.

ben Zion, Ilan. *How Herod the Tyrant Saved the Olympics.* The Times of Israel, 7 Feb 2014.

Bond, Sarah. *A Brief History of Olympic Nudity from Ancient Greece to ESPN.* Forbes.com, 8 Apr 2016.

Bookidis, Nancy. "*The Sanctuaries of Corinth,*" *Corinth, Vol.20.* Athens: The American School of Classical Studies at Athens, 2003.

Brenton, Sir Lancelot C.L. *The Septuagint with Apocrypha: Greek and English.* London: Samuel Bagster, 1851.

Britannica, The Editors of Encyclopaedia. "*Roman Road System.*" Encyclopaedia Britannica, 3 Apr 2018, *https://britannica.com/technology/Roman-road-system.* Accessed 10 Mar 2021.

Britannica, The Editors of Encyclopaedia. "*Sibylline Oracles.*" Encyclopaedia Britannica, 8 May 2020, *https://britannica.com/topic/Sibylline-Oracles.* Accessed 10 Mar 2021.

Bruce, F.F. *The Epistle to the Hebrews: The New International Commentary of the New Testament.* Grand Rapids: Wm. B Eerdmans, 1964.

Bruce, F.F. *New Testament History.* New York: Doubleday, 1980.

Cadbury, H.J. "The Macellum of Corinth," *Journal of Biblical Literature,* Vol. 53, No. 2, Jul 1934.

Conybeare, W.J. and J.S.Howson. *The Life and Epistles of St. Paul.* New York: Charles Scribner, 1855.

Deissmann, Adolf. *Light from the Ancient East*. New York: George H. Doran, 1927.

Denney, James. *St Paul's Epistle to the Romans, The Expositor's Greek Testament*. London: Hodder and Stoughton, 1903.

Drozdek, Adam. *Acta Antiqua Academiae Scientiarum Hungariae*. AK Journals, Vol. 45, Issue 1, 2005.

Edersheim, Alfred. *The Life and Times of Jesus the Messiah*. New York: Longmans, Green & Co, 1912.

Elwell, Walter A. *Baker Commentary on the Bible*. Grand Rapids: Baker, 1989.

Evelyn-White, Hugh. *Hesiod, the Homeric Hymns and Homerica*. London: William Heinemann, 1920.

Findlay, G.G. *St. Paul's First Epistle to the Corinthians, The Expositor's Greek Testament*. London: Hodder and Stroughton, 1903.

Fant, Clyde E. and Mitchell G. Reddish. *A Guide to Biblical Sites in Greece and Turkey*. New York: Oxford University Press, 2003.

Furneaux, William M. *The Acts of the Apostles*. Oxford: Claredon Press, 1912.

Godet, Frederic. *Commentary on First Corinthians*. Grand Rapids: Kregel, 1977.

Godet, Frederic. *Commentary on Romans*. Grand Rapids: Kregel, 1977.

Hastings, James. *Hastings Dictionary of the Bible*. New York: Charles Scribner's, 1909.

Hellenic Ministry of Culture. *St. Paul's Prison: Philippi*. Athens: Archaeological Receipts Fund.

Hesiod, *Theogony*, 8th-7th century BC.

Hodge, Charles. *Commentary on the Epistle to the Romans*. Grand Rapids: Eerdmans, 1972.

Hodgkin, A.M. *Christ in All the Scriptures*. London: Pickering & Inglis, 1907.

Homer. *The Iliad*. 8th century BC.

Homer. *The Odyssey*. 8th century BC.

Homer. *Homeric Hymns*. 7th century BC.

Hooker, M.A. *The Use of Sibyls and Sibylline Oracles in Early Christian Writers*. Cincinnati: University of Cincinnati, 2007.

Horace. *Book 2, Epistle 1*. 1st Century BC.

Hornblower, Simon and Anthony Spawforth, Editors. *The Oxford Classical Dictionary*. Oxford: Oxford University Press, 2003.

Isocrates. *Αρεοπαγιτικός*. 5th–4th century BC.

Jamieson, Robert, Andrew Faussett and David Brown. *Commentary on the Whole Bible*. Grand Rapids: Zondervan.

Jeffers, James S. *The Greco-Roman World of the New Testament Era.* Downers Grove, IL: InterVarsity Press, 1999.

Kern, Otto. *Eleusinische Beiträge, (Eleusian Contributions).* Halle, Germany: Buchdruckerei des Waisenhauses, 1909.

Kittel, Gerhard. *Theological Dictionary of the New Testament.* Grand Rapids: Eerdmans, 1964.

Leake, William H. *Travels in The Morea with a Map and Plans.* London: John Murray, 1830.

Lenski, R.C.H. *The Interpretation of the Acts of the Apostles.* Minneapolis: Augsburg Publishing House, 1961.

Lewis, C.S. *Is Theology Poetry? The Socratic Digest*, Vol.3. Oxford: University Press, 1945.

Liddell, Henry and Robert Scott. *Greek-English Lexicon Abridged.* New York: American Book Company, 1871.

Longnecker, Richard N. *The Acts of the Apostles, The Expositor's Bible Commentary.* Grand Rapids: Zondervan, 1981.

Macgregor, G.H.C. *Acts, The Interpreter's Bible*, Vol. 9. New York: Abingdon Press, 1954.

Marshall, I. Howard. *The Acts of the Apostles: Tyndale New Testament Commentaries.* Grand Rapids: Wm. B Eerdmans, 1980.

McDonnel, Myles. *Athletic Nudity among Greeks and Etruscans: The Evidence of the "Perizoma Vases."* Rome: École Française de Rome, 1993.

Metzger, Bruce M. *The Language of the New Testament, The Interpreter's Bible*, Vol. 7. New York: Abingdon Press, 1951.

Meyer, H.A.W. *The Acts of the Apostles.* New York: Funk & Wagnalls, 1883.

Mounce, William D. and Robert H. Mounce. *Greek and English Interlinear New Testament.* Grand Rapids: Zondervan, 2008.

Murphy-O'Connor, Jerome. *St. Paul's Corinth: Text and Archaeology.* Collegeville, MN: Liturgical Press, 2002.

MVSEI VATICANI. www.museivaticani.va

Parmenides. *On Nature.* 5th century BC.

Pausanias. *Description of Greece.* 2nd century AD.

Pelekanidou, Elli S. *The Traditional Prison of Apostle Paul.* Archaeological Announcement (1st Local Symposium: "Kavala and the Environs.") Thessaloniki: 1980.

Plato. *Apology.* 399 BC.

Plato. *Symposium.* 4th century BC.

Plato. *Theaetetus.* 4th century BC.

Plutarch. *Aristides*. 1st Century AD.

Plutarch. *Περί των Έκλελοιπότων Χρηστηρίων*. 1st century AD.

Plutarch. *Parallel Lives*. 1st Century AD.

Rackham, Richard B. *The Acts of the Apostles*. London: Methuen & Co, 1901.

Richardson, Don. *Eternity in Their Hearts*. Ventura, CA: Regal Books, 1981.

Robertson, A.T. *Word Pictures in the New Testament*. Nashville: Broadman Press, 1930.

Rowdon, Harold H. *The International Bible Commentary*. Grand Rapids: Zondervan, 1986.

Sanday, William and Arthur C. Headlam. *The Epistle to the Romans, The International Critical Commentary*, New York: Charles Scribner's Sons, 1896.

Schaff, Philip. *History of the Christian Church*. New York: Charles Scribner's Sons, 1889.

Singer, Isador. *The Jewish Encyclopedia*. Vol. II. New York: Funk & Wagnalls, 1907.

Strabo. *Geography*, 1st century AD.

Swete, H.B. *The Ascended Christ*. London: MacMillan, 1912.

Tenney, Merrill C. *New Testament Survey*. Grand Rapids: Eerdmans, 1961.

Thirlwall, Connop. *A History of Greece*. New York: Harper & Brothers, 1845.

Thompson, Homer A. *The Stoa of Attalos II in Athens*. The American School of Classical Studies in Athens. Lunenburg, VT: Stinehour Press, 1992.

Thucydides. *The History of the Peloponnesian War II* (Pericles Funeral Oration). 431 BC.

Torrey, R.A. *The Higher Criticism and the New Theology: Unscientific, Unscriptural and Unwholesome*. New York: Gospel Publishing House, 1911.

Trench, Richard Chenevix. *Synonyms of the New Testament*. London: MacMillan and Co, 1880.

Vincent, Marvin R. *Word Studies in the New Testament*. Grand Rapids: Eerdman's Publishing, 1946.

Vine, W.E. *Vine's Expository Dictionary of Old and New Testament Words*. Nashville: Thomas Nelson, 1997.

Washburn, Oliver M. *The Charioteer of Delphi*. American Journal of Archaeology. Vol. X, Number 2. New York: Macmillan, 1906.

Westcott, B.F. *The Gospel According to St. John*. Cambridge, 1881.

Wright, N.T. *Paul for Everyone: Romans*. Part 2. Louisville: Westminster John Knox Press, 2004.

Verse Index

Greek Words

English Word	Transliteration	Greek Word	Page
Aeropagus	AR'EIOS PAG'OS	Αρειος Πάγος	156
Blessed	MAKAR'IOS	μακάριος	84
Body	SOM'A	σώμα	134
Bought	AGORA'ZO	'αγοράζο	184
Church	EKKLESI'A	'εκκλησια	144
City authorities	POLITAR'CHES	πολιτάρχης	66
Colony	KOLONI'A	κολωηία	40
Cover	KATAKALYP'TO	κατακαλύπτω	180
Departed from	CHORI'ZO	χωρίζω 'εκ	162
Diadem	DIAD'EMA	διάδημα	68
Discipline	HYPOPIA'ZO	ύπωπιάζω	112
Divination	PY'THON	Πύθων	54
Fix our gaze upon	APHORA'O	'αφοράω	116
Fortune-telling	MANTEUO'MAI	μαντεύομαι	110
Friend	PHI'LOS	φίλος	150
Gates	PY'LE	πύλη	88
Good	AGATHOS'	'αλαθός	152
in Greek	HELLENISTI'	'Ελληνιστί	26
Hades	HA'DES	'άδης	82
Holy	HAG'IOS	άγιον	106
Image	EICON'	είκών	98
Impediment	OG'KOS	'όγκος	114
Imperishable	APH'THARTOS	'άφθαρτοζ	72
Judgment seat	BE'MA	βήμα	48
King	BASIL'EUS	βασιλεύς	20

English Word	Transliteration	Greek Word	Page
Leopard	PAR'DALIS	παρδάλις	24
Lord	KY'RIOS	κύριος	56
Lot	KLER'OS	κλῆρος	140
Love	AGAPĀ'O	'αγαπαω	104
Macedonia	MAKEDON'IA	Μακεδονία	36
Magistrates	STRATEGOS'	στρατηγός	50
Man	ANTH'ROPOS	'άνθρωπος	22
Marketplace	AGORA'	'αγορά	46,132
Meat market	MAKEL'LON	μάκελλον	194
Mystery	MYSTE'RION	μυστήριον	166
Nations	ETH'NOS	'έθνος	16
Outsider	IDIOT'ES	'ιδιώτες	136
Parable	PARABOLE'	παραβολή	168
Partaker	KOINONOS'	κοινωνός	86
Passed by	DIODEU'O	διοδεύω	64
Passed judgment on	KRI'NO	κρίνω	142
Pillar	STY'LOS	στῦλος	130
Portico	STO'A	στοά	158
Preach the gospel	EUANGELI'ZO	εύαγγελίζω	38
Priest	HEIRUS'	ίερεύς	20
Prison	PHULAKE'	φυλακή	52
Proconsul	ANTHY'PATOS	'ανθύπατος	118
Prophet	PROPHE'TES	προφήτης	108
Prostitute	POR'NE	πόρνη	178
Resurrection	ANASTA'SIS	'ανάστασις	154
Revelation	APOKAL'YPSIS	'αποκάλυψις	170
Sash	ZO'NE	ζώνη	120
Scroll	BIBLI'ON	βιβλίον	78
Seek	ZETE'O	ζητέω	18
Seller of purple	PORPHUROP'OLIS	πορφυρόπωλις	42

English Word	Transliteration	Greek Word	Page
Servant	DIAK'ONOS	διάκονοξ	200
Servant	DOU'LOS	δοῦλος	58
Speak	LALE'O	λαλέω	186
Speech	LO'GOS	λόγος	138
Spiritual	PNEUMATIKOS'	πνευματικός	196
Standing	HIS'TEMI	'ίστημι	160
Stone Pavement	LITHOSTRO'TOS	λιθόστρωτοσ	190
Stronghold	OCHU'ROMA	ὀχύρωμα	192
Synagogue	SYNAGOGE'	συναγωγή	76
Theater	THE'ATRON	θέατρον	44
Treasurer	OIKONOM'OS	οίκονόμος	182
Tribunal	BE'MA	βῆμα	188
Triumphing over	THRIAMBEU'O	θριαμβεύω	198
Unknown	AG'NOSTOS	'άγνωστος	146
Warned	CHRĒMATI'ZŌ	χρηματίζω	104
Way	HOSDOS'	όδός	148
Wheat	SI'TOS	σῖτος	172
Wilderness	ER'EMOS	'έρημος	92
Wisdom	SOPHI'A	σοφία	126
With	PROS'	πρός	128
Work	ERGAZ'OMAI	'εργάζομαι	96
Wreath	STEPH'ANOS	στέφανος	70